coldplay

NOBODY SAID IT WAS EASY

Cover & Book designed by Fresh Lemon.
Picture research by Sarah Bacon.

ISBN: 0.7119.9810.8
Order No: OP 49412

Exclusive Distributors
Music Sales Limited,
8/9 Frith Street, London W1D 3JB, UK.

Music Sales Corporation,
257 Park Avenue South, New York, NY 10010, USA.

Macmillan Distribution Services,
53 Park West Drive, Derrimut, Vic 3030, Australia.

To the Music Trade only:
Music Sales Limited,
8/9 Frith Street, London W1D 3JB, UK.

Photo credits:
Allover Press/Rex Features: 69; David Atlas/RetnaUK: 89;
Thomas Dubois/RetnaUK: 63; Robin Francois/RetnaUK: 58;
Dave Hogan/Rex Features: 86; LFI: 1, 2, 3, 5, 6, 7, 12, 13, 15, 17, 20, 22, 25,
27, 34, 37, 38, 43, 51, 52, 55, 56, 60, 67, 70, 72, 76, 78, 79, 80, 83, 91, 93,
94, 95, 96, 99, 100, 111, 112, 113, 114, 116, 120, 123, 124, 125, 126, 128;
Tony Motts/SIN: 8; Andrew Murray/Rex Features: 108;
Alessio Pizzicannella/SIN: 44, 47; Brian Rasic/Rex Features: 75;
Rex Features: 117; Robin/RetnaUK: 10, 48; Simon Runting/Rex Features: 119;
Roy Tee/SIN: 32; Richard Young/Rex Features: 64
Colour Section: Alessio Pizzicannella/SIN/Corbis: 1; Steve Gillett: 2 (main pic), 5;
LFI: 2, 4; Roy Tee/SIN: 3

Every effort has been made to trace the copyright holders of the
photographs in this book but one or two were unreachable.
We would be grateful if the photographers concerned would contact us.

Printed by: Printwise (Haverhill) Limited, Suffolk, Great Britain

A catalogue record for this book is available from the British Library.

Visit Omnibus Press on the web at www.omnibuspress.com

coldplay

NOBODY SAID IT WAS EASY

MARTIN ROACH

OMNIBUS PRESS

LONDON / NEW YORK / PARIS / SYDNEY / COPENHAGEN / BERLIN / MADRID / TOKYO

CONTENTS

INTRODUCTION

Among the more fascinating aspects of the music industry is its ability to produce the unpredictable. At a time when the naysayers have made a career bemoaning the death of originality and invention in music, tired as they are of an endless tide of pop wannabees, there was always the chance that a band would crop up that defied the fashion, went against the grain and provided the exception that may prove the rule. Coldplay is just such a band.

Alternately described as "the new U2/Travis/Radiohead" et al, or "knobhead students/bedwetters", Coldplay have the ability to frustrate and delight in equal measure. Their recorded output has justifiably enjoyed critical plaudits that few bands could dream of, quickly matched by mammoth commercial success. Yet their moral stance on numerous issues has attracted its fair share of largely undue criticism – as indeed has their reclusive approach to life as a modern rock band.

The centre of Coldplay's world is undoubtedly Chris Martin, its principal songwriter, lead singer and visual presence. Despite his avowed revulsion to the cult of celebrity, in a few short years his band's meteoric success has thrust him unwittingly into an intense media spotlight, bringing with it an inevitable flurry of rumour and gossip. His apparent fragility and lack of confidence might seem to contradict his acclaimed musical talent, but this same insecurity is the very fuel to Coldplay's fire. Without this, the band would probably not exist, at least not in the form that we know.

How they came from nowhere to become one of the world's biggest bands is a story centred mostly around their stunning catalogue of music, but also one that takes in Hollywood actresses, internal disputes, frequent uncertainty about the their future and high profile music biz spats. Nonetheless, they have emerged triumphant, newly crowned as rock's latest saviours. How did they do it? Is it justified? Will they be able to maintain this lofty status? Read on...

CHAPTER 1:

WINNERS AND LOSERS IN COOL BRITANNIA

"We were thinking about this yesterday - we were just sitting in a little room (at college), just writing songs all the time. And then three years later we can play them all over the world." **Chris Martin**

It's the autumn of 1996, and music of wildly contrasting integrity clutters up the British charts. For those with discerning ears, there was the chart-topping 'Setting Sun' by The Chemical Brothers featuring Noel Gallagher, followed a few weeks later by 'Breathe', a hard dance masterpiece by the world-conquering Prodigy. Yet over on the album charts, the run-in to Christmas saw a terrifying sequence at the top, starting with Peter Andre, followed by Simply Red, Beautiful South, Boyzone, The Spice Girls and, more disturbing still, Robson & Jerome, chart-topping at Christmas for the second year in succession.

The year had started off well with Oasis' *(What's The Story) Morning Glory?*, a multi-platinum album and the logical commercial peak of the self-styled Britpop movement. Genealogically traceable through Suede's London-centric first album and still further back through the so-called New Wave of New Wave bands, Britpop was a welcome respite from the slacker culture and US-dominated grunge years at the start of the decade. At its height, Britpop saw an eighteen-month heyday when Blur and Oasis were household names; Pulp finally break their fourteen-year duck with the sexually subversive, comically seedy triumph *His 'n' Hers*; and Elastica, The Auteurs and the soon-to-be-global Radiohead all making impacts. Supergrass' debut album *I Should Coco* hit number one and a litany of other bands enjoyed purple patches as well, including Shed Seven, Portishead, The Bluetones, Marion, Dodgy and even a revived Modfather, Paul Weller, who smiled benignly down on these young disciples who'd obviously listened hard to The Jam's back catalogue. It was good for business too, with live music experiencing a resurgence, band merchandise selling out and festivals enjoying renewed popularity.

NOEL GALLAGHER - OASIS

By 1996, however, Britpop's foundations were crumbling. All was not well in the camp. The 'chart battle' between Oasis and the triumphant Blur the previous August had seen Britpop's commercial zenith but, paradoxically, its creative nadir. Despite their fleeting chart success, Blur soon took second place to Oasis' coming behemoth album, leaving Damon Albarn to shrink into a corner, reviled by the cartoon excesses of his band and distrusted for being Britpop's pretty boy. Within five years, the man who frolicked with Page Three stunners in the video for 'Country House' was recording world music with African instrumentalists.

For the Gallaghers, 'Roll With It' was arguably their worst single ever, which Noel as much as admitted in later interviews. Seeing both bands on *The Six O'Clock News* seemed a portent of halcyon days gone by. Britpop had been picked up by the media as a perfect counterpoint to the tiresome machismo - and corporate mutation - of grunge. Now, within two years of Kurt Cobain's suicide, Britpop had turned into the monster it had once despised. By mid-1996, with most of the big Britpop players recording new material and on sabbaticals, the movement was effectively dead.

A few survivors floated to the surface in the post-Britpop vacuum. Suede negotiated the loss of their guitarist and returned with *Coming Up*, an album which may not have enjoyed the critical and commercial acclaim of previous records but was clearly their best effort to date. Manic Street Preachers were already well on the way to stadium status, though many felt this was achieved on the back of increasingly conservative output. Blur's forthcoming hardcore-inspired eponymous album was a dramatic shift in direction that firmly refuted their Britpop tag.

Britpop was never a transatlantic phenomenon. Ironic, quirky vignettes by bands like Blur, Suede, Bluetones, Supergrass, Pulp and a host of others meant nothing in America. Oasis enjoyed some *Billboard* success but this was diminished by unseemly tiffs between the brothers Gallagher and disrupted tours that prevented any real momentum being generated. Radiohead, almost throttled by the unexpected success of the anthem 'Creep', had pulled back from the brink with the delicious subtleties of *The Bends* but would not enjoy global popularity until the seismic impact of their pivotal *OK Computer*. Only The Prodigy, who entered the *Billboard* chart at No. 1 with *Fat Of The Land* (as they did in 23 other countries compared to *Morning Glory*'s fourteen) could boast truly international success but the Essex hard dance band fell way outside the shadow of Britpop.

What, pop-pickers wanted to know, would happen next?

DAMON ALBAN - BLUR

It was against this backdrop, in the uneasy calm of the post-Britpop vacuum, that the four future members of Coldplay began to assemble. The traction beam for many aspiring rock stars is London and the capital duly sucked them all in, heady with dreams of stardom and musical acclaim.

Chris Martin was the eldest son of a chartered accountant father and a mother who taught biology. Born on March 3, 1977, he shares his birthday with Alexander Graham Bell, the inventor of the telephone. That same month, A&M were reneging on the record deal they had famously signed with The Sex Pistols outside Buckingham Palace, a contract which so shocked Rick Wakeman that the caped Yes-man threatened to withdraw his labour. Punk captured the headlines while disco dominated the dancefloor; artists like Donna Summer, Showaddywaddy, Hot Chocolate and The Muppets enjoyed far more commercial success than punk's angry firebrands.

The anti-establishment rants of London's punk inner circle was far removed from the sleepy Devonshire village of Whitestone, a few miles east of Exeter, where Chris was born. He was raised with his four siblings: two sisters, one thirteen years his junior and another who works as a nurse in Birmingham; and two brothers, one still a teenager today, the other just one year Chris' junior who is now an aspiring drum 'n' bass DJ in Manchester. In light of Chris' latterday reputation as an almost puritanical abstainer, this brother was apparently just the opposite: "(He is) the anti-Chris, the cool one (who has) experienced all these things for me." Prior to Chris, the nearest the Martin family had come to fame was his great-great-grandfather, William Willet, who invented British summertime. While riding his horse early each morning, Willet rued the fact that no one else was enjoying the sunshine and came up with the simple brainwave to move the clocks forward one hour.

The family home was large and set in luxuriant grounds. Chris spent much of his childhood gazing out of sash windows across manicured lawns, and he makes no secret of the fact that he benefited from a first-class education. His secondary studies sent him to Sherborne boarding school in Yeovil, one of the country's finest public schools. A battered comprehensive this may not have been, but there was certainly no shortage of opportunities for creativity. Chris was a keen artist, but his primary love was always music. He had mixed tastes at this stage – the first single he bought was Blur's 'There's no Other Way' and the first album was Michael Jackson's 40 million seller, *Thriller*. He also had a penchant for The Pet Shop Boys and a smattering of soul classics.

"What was I like as a kid? The same as I am now, just smaller with a higher voice" CHRIS MARTIN

Inevitably, his passion for listening to records evolved into a need to play music himself. In very early bands he played keyboards only alongside various school friends, bands subsequently identified as The Rockin' Honkies and The Red Rooster Boogie Band, who counted standards such as 'Mustang Sally' and 'Sitting On The Dock Of The Bay' as key tracks in their set.

Another early band was The Pet Shop Boys-influenced Identity Crisis. Although short-lived, this electro-pop outfit did provide one essential experience which Chris Martin would carry into his adulthood and career with Coldplay: being booed offstage. Already Chris had taken to the stage in a less-than-flattering leather waistcoat, video footage of which is said to be locked deep in some ex-pupil's wardrobe. However, his sartorial faux pas worsened. At one particular gig, Chris borrowed a long raincoat from a friend and enthusiastically aped the rock star antics of U2's frontman Bono. It went down like the proverbial lead balloon. Distraught, Chris vowed to only ever "be completely normal" from then on. Fortunately, all was not lost. Through a shared love of U2's *Zooropa* Chris met Phil Harvey, Coldplay's future manager and 'fifth member' of the band. They quickly became close friends, and Chris even dated Phil's younger sister for a while.

Back at home, Chris' musical bent was readily encouraged by his father, although his dad later admitted that he was just humouring him in the hope that the phase would pass. Inadvertently of course, this just fuelled Chris' enthusiasm.

In later years, Chris' father proved to be one of the band's biggest fans and his son's most sage advisor.

His father's encouragement was mirrored by an open-minded music teacher at Chris' school, Mr Tanner. "He dismissed the idea that you had to be some kind of miniature Mozart to enjoy music," says Chris. "He bought these Yamaha keyboards for the school, those PSS140s, about £100. They were very easy to work with, everyone could have a go. You could play with one finger and have a tune, so we did. That led to the first band I was in."

Outside of music, Chris' time at Sherbourne was largely unremarkable. The most troublesome period in his eyes was when, for a couple of years, he worried he was gay and fretted about the barracking and prejudice he might suffer: "I was sixteen

CHRIS MARTIN

when I finally felt confident I wasn't (gay). But the homophobia (at public school) can be pretty intense." There was even one time when he spotted a girl who he thought looked nice, but when she turned around it was a boy. "So I put on a deep voice and walked away!"

Probably the most controversial episode in Chris' otherwise sedate teenage years was when he and a friend stole a Mars Bar from Superdrug and got caught – although he never did it again, so he was hardly a juvenile repeat offender. He was much happier reading Sherlock Holmes stories, surfing and listening to obscure classical piano music.

With the security of Coldplay's near-universal critical acclaim to ease his inner doubts, Chris can now be more forthright about his childhood years: "I hate apologising because as far as I'm concerned it was a privilege to have an amazing education. I had some incredible teachers, great facilities. What a privilege! But so what? Does anyone give a shit?"

Fife, Scotland-born Guy Berryman was the son of an engineer and, like Chris, also came from a stable household of means. The first dozen years of his childhood were spent in Kirkaldy, before a family relocation to Canterbury in Kent when he was thirteen. Like most primary school children, Guy started learning the recorder aged only eight, then progressed on to trumpet and finally, the year he moved to Kent, the bass. He began dabbling in numerous school bands, most notably the hideously named Time Out, an outfit that specialised in Genesis covers. "It was guitar and keyboards band," he recalled. "We played terrible, terrible stuff. The best musician in the group was really into Genesis. We would agonise for hours trying to work out horrible prog rock stuff with ridiculous solos. We never got anywhere near it – we'd muck about and make a noise."

Time Out's questionable set list was in marked contrast to Guy's own musical preferences which were decidedly funk and R&B-flavoured. He admits to having paid £100 for a rare vinyl copy of James Brown's *Hell* album only to see it re-issued on CD for £12 a few weeks later. "A bit annoying, but I did get an old Kool & The Gang compilation at a car-boot sale for 50p, which is worth £60. I just love that stuff, the rawness and the energy." He says his funk and soul collection was selected by follicle grandeur rather than musical preferences, with the young bassist selecting most of his purchases by the size of Afro haircuts on the record sleeve.

Southampton-born Will Champion was the son of music teacher parents and therefore a more adept musician than his band cohorts, even at an early age. By his own admission, he was a far from ideal primary school pupil and ended up at a rough comprehensive for his secondary years. According to Will, fellow school mates 'graduated' to numerous prison sentences for, among other things, kicking somebody to death, GBH, arson and rape. So much for a privileged education. However, he believes he would have hated public school and feels the more abrasive environment at his school at least made him more street-wise.

The only known band from Will's childhood was called Fat Hamster. Will was proficient on many different instruments, including the ever-useful tin whistle, so his latter-day decision to switch from guitar to drums was not as great a leap of faith as it might appear. "Will is like a human jukebox," explained Chris. "He knows more songs than anyone. You name it, he'll play it."

Jon Buckland came from Mold, a working class area of Clywd in north Wales, whose only rock and roll claim to fame were former residents The Alarm, Karl Wallinger of World Party and Hollywood Brit-actor Rhys Ifans. Jon was born to a music-teacher mother and a biology/chemistry teacher father. Jon's father adored Eric Clapton and Jimi Hendrix so his son's role in Coldplay is not surprising.

Jon can play the piano and harmonica (like Chris) and started learning guitar two years earlier than Guy, aged only eleven. One year prior to that, he'd formed an ad hoc rap band, but this outfit quickly mutated into a pop act, which was how he came to be interested in guitar. He could lay claim to perhaps the most critically acceptable of childhood influences, preferring guitar bands such as The Stone Roses and Ride. Add to the mix a splice of his older brother's My Bloody Valentine and Sonic Youth records and the young guitarist already had an intriguing blend of influences. The first two records he recalls buying were rather less impressive: a Beautiful South single and the mega-mix musical horror that was the chart-topping Jive Bunny & The Master Mixers.

Jon's first guitar was a simple, budget, Japanese six-string. He tried to form bands pretty soon after he had mastered the rudiments of the instrument. His early teenage years were mostly a mass of badly drawn album covers for non-existent bands with increasingly corny names. One heavy metal band which did make it to actual rehearsals played a bizarre cover of Madness' classic, 'Night Boat To Cairo'.

WILL CHAMPION, GUY BERRYMAN & JON BUCKLAND

The hub of Coldplay's genesis was University College, London. The product of four decidedly unbroken homes, the future members of Coldplay all headed for the central London school with unashamed aspirations for a bright future: "(We all had) real Dick Whittington-type ambitions," admitted Chris. "Go to London, make your fortune. Well, sort of. And when you go to college you've got a clean slate, no-one knows who you are and you've kind of decided pretty much who you want to be."

Will enrolled for an Anthropology course (his father was an archaeologist once described by Chris as "the Michael Jackson of archaeology"); Jon opted for Maths and Astronomy; Guy followed in his father's footsteps by studying Engineering, although he later switched to Architecture; for Chris, the process was a little more protracted. At first he applied to another college to study English but was politely informed that his stated wish, as stated on his application form, that he wanted to improve his written language "to help with my lyrics" was not what they were looking for. Eventually, Chris ended up at UCL studying Ancient History.

The first Freshers' week saw Chris and Jon become acquainted around the Students' Union pool table. They became friends and shared a common interest in music, albeit Sting and a then-disco obsessed and critically chided U2. The other music Chris began to hear at UCL was a revelation, however, and before long he was tumbling into the expressive vocals and staggering range of the late Jeff Buckley. In turn, Buckley's renowned diversity in his selection of covers led Chris into buying albums by artists as varied as Leonard Cohen and Elkie Brooks. Closer to home, the increasingly perplexing yet utterly compelling genius of Radiohead was also a regular on the stereo during Chris and Jon's late night halls of residence hang-outs, as were epic throwbacks from the likes of Echo & The Bunnymen.

Undeterred by the lack of a full band or any live experience together, the duo immediately started writing original material. "Meeting Jonny was like falling in love. He could make all the ideas work and we were writing two songs a night sometimes." Jon was reciprocally impressed: "From the moment I met Chris, I really did think that we could go all the way."

For the next nine months, Chris and Jon toyed with formally starting a band, cobbling together snippets of songs and ideas for music while all the time continuing their studies. Rumour has it that Chris was even formulating a boy band as his route to musical glory, an outfit whose name - Pectoralz - promised little in the way of Grammy-winning creative genius. Fortunately, events took a turn that would ensure Pectoralz remained just a bad pipe dream (or so Chris would have us believe). Legend has it that fellow UCL student and funk-obsessed bassist Guy Berryman heard of Chris and Jon's embryonic compositions and confronted them in the student bar, inebriatedly demanding to be allowed to join their 'band'. "We couldn't really say no," recalls Jon. Chris thought that Guy was a little scary when they first met but now says he is much nicer than he appears, being softly-spoken rather than moody, albeit still the "dark member" of Coldplay.

Shortly after, Guy dropped out of his engineering course, opting instead for a degree in architecture that was supposed to span a full seven years. He eventually pulled out of that too but opted to stay in London to see how this new band with Chris and Jon worked out (leaving Guy as the only non-graduate in the band). Just as well, because by the time he would have finished the seven-year course and begun the lucrative work of being a qualified architect, he was already part of one of the biggest bands on the planet with a clutch of Brits, two Grammys and millions of records sold.

All three band mates lived in UCL's Ramsey Hall, their close proximity to each other making it easy to strum guitars and write songs whenever it took their fancy. With a student aplomb that would appall their later critics, the trio would often find themselves playing Simon & Garfunkel songs in the stairwells of the halls of residence.

The final piece of the Coldplay jigsaw was the arrival of Will Champion. The nature of his recruitment as permanent drummer was quite the opposite to that of the overtly enthusiastic bassist Guy. The trio of Chris, Jon and Guy knew of a reputable drummer at UCL and approached him with a crude demo of some nascent songs, which included a very early version of Coldplay's eventual début album opener, 'Don't Panic'. "We played him 'Panic' and he said, 'No'. We just couldn't believe it. Even then there was a feeling of, 'But what we're doing is great. Why wouldn't you want to be part of it?'"

One day, Chris was recounting this rejection to his hockey team-mate and casual acquaintance, Will Champion. Will informed Chris that his room-mate was a drummer and offered to set up a rehearsal. The problem was, when the three arrived at Will's digs, the drummer was nowhere to be seen. Anxious not to have wasted their time, Will suggested that, although he was actually an aspiring guitarist, maybe he could keep basic time behind the kit and they could rehearse anyway. With the absent drummer down the local pub, Will thus found himself enrolled as Coldplay's sticksman. The date was January 6, 1998.

Coldplay "borrowed" their name from a fellow student who no longer wanted to use the moniker because he felt it was "too depressing". Just as well, as alternative names that had been mooted were Stepney Green or Starfish - there are unsubstantiated rumours of them playing an actual gig in Camden under the latter name.

The first ever 'official' Coldplay song was a novelty number called 'Ode To Deodorant', compiled in Jon's bedroom. At this stage, it wasn't just their songs that were far from rock star material: Chris was shy, lanky and wore a tooth brace, hardly a nineteen-year-old potential Kurt Cobain.

Will proved more than just a useful stand-in drummer. He handed over his blue Telecaster to Jon, and the same guitar went on to provide the backbone to many Coldplay songs. Then, within a few days of stumbling into the band, he arranged a gig at the now-defunct Laurel Tree in Camden, north London. Among the six song set, nervously aired to a modest crowd made up almost entirely of college mates, were two songs, 'Don't Panic' and 'High Speed', which - suitably honed – would made it on to the début album. Quite how these ethereal ballads, in particular the softly-spoken chimes of the latter, came across over the house PA of a small pub is lost in the mists of time. Yet even in Coldplay's infancy, Chris recalls that the band had grand designs that made no countenance for failure: "There was no Plan B."

CHAPTER 2:

SAFETY IN NUMBERS

With the world's attention drawn to the football World Cup in France, Coldplay developed their masterplan. First priority was songwriting, closely followed by almost daily rehearsals in bathrooms, cellars, bedrooms, and even one wind-swept session in a local park.

The band's manager arrived courtesy of a mix-up over a gig. They had arranged to play at Dingwalls in Camden, persuading the venue to put two friends' bands on the bill as well. Coach loads of mates were chaperoned to come to the show and Coldplay spent weeks avidly rehearsing.

Then two weeks before the actual gig, it became clear there had been a big mix-up. There were actually going to be eight bands on the bill, Coldplay were on fifth and would play for only fifteen minutes. They would get no door money and just 10p for each flyer handed in with their name on it.

Chris had kept in touch with his friend Phil Harvey, a fellow pupil at Sherbourne and in the midst of this impending disaster, asked him outright to be their manager. Phil agreed and immediately phoned up Dingwalls to cancel the gig. He then cleverly hired out the same venue - with his own money - the night after Coldplay had originally been booked. Not only that, he offered to pay for the band to go into a tiny studio called Sync City, in Tottenham, to record their first demo.

The princely sum of £1,500 was needed for this first recording. It was spring 1998 and the singles charts were peppered by the likes of Aqua, Boyzone, B★Witched and All Saints. Massive Attack had just enjoyed a number one with their 'comeback' album *Mezzanine* but otherwise the British music scene was largely unrewarding.

The product of this début studio session was *The Safety EP*. It contained three tracks, the subtle swagger of 'Bigger Stronger', 'No More Keeping My Feet On The Ground' and 'Such A Rush'. All three songs had Jon's trademark ringing guitars and Chris' gentle voice, but this was very much a less refined version of Coldplay than would be found on later records. Still, it was a strong opening salvo intended merely as a sampler for record companies and music industry only. Interestingly, the name of the EP actually comes from the sleeve itself – the cover photograph was a long exposure shot of Chris standing under a doorway 'Safety' sign. Phil Harvey had taken to the role of band manager with a passion and worked relentlessly to spread the gospel with this début release.

Without an orthodox record deal or even a self-distribution deal, the limited edition of only 500 copies of *The Safety EP* was destined for the record collections of friends and a few select members of the media and record business. It is now one of the most sought after releases for any Coldplay record collector, with scarce copies occasionally appearing on e-bay for in excess of £150.

At this point, gigs were scarce, especially throughout the football-obsessed summer months of 1998. What gigs they did secure invariably ended up in chaos. Coldplay performed at Wye Farming College's end of term ball, billed as support to then-chart regulars Space. Countless technical problems meant Space eventually played *first* at 11pm, followed by two other bands before Coldplay finally took to the stage at 3am. By this time, most people were either blind drunk or dog-tired. One member of the audience kept getting up on stage and dancing alongside the band, before returning to his corner of the room for another swig of watery student beer.

Coldplay's next live disaster was at Manchester's unsigned band festival, 'In The City'. This September gig at the Cuban Café got off to a bad start when Chris left his guitar pedals in Devon. Phil did a spot of quick thinking and arranged for a long distance lorry driver he knew to take the pedals up to Manchester as part of his route. Coldplay were the first band on at the miniscule venue, circumstances made worse by a soundman who patently detested Coldplay's sound and wanted only to drink beer. Chris forgot the words to the first song and matters went downhill from there on.

All of these early live experiences were solicited by *The Safety EP*. Although they were far from enjoyable, they were an essential part of the band's apprenticeship. On December 7, 1998, however, the EP secured them a gig that would prove to be pivotal. The show was at the Camden Falcon pub, a small but legendary venue that had seen famously crammed gigs by the likes of Suede, Blur, PJ Harvey and many others 'before they were famous'. The pub was a regular haunt for record company A&R men.

> "I wasn't really that enamoured, I thought Chris had something. He was quite charismatic. But the sound wasn't there"

At the Falcon that night was Simon Williams, some time music journalist and now founder of the independent record label, Fierce Panda. Williams was sufficiently impressed to approach Coldplay with a one-off single deal. He also named the band as one of his tips for success in the New Year's edition of *NME*, despite still being unsigned. Anyone intrigued by his festive tip-off was able to see them play live during a New Year smattering of small pub circuit shows in January, including two dates at the Bull & Gate in Kentish Town.

Coldplay signed with Fierce Panda and immediately recorded 'Brothers And Sisters', b/w 'Easy To Please' and 'Only Superstition', which was released in April, 1999. Although only 2,500 copies were pressed, the more accomplished sound soon began to make ripples in the music business. For a start, the band enjoyed their first music press reviews, most notably perhaps in *NME*, who said the song "has a clear eye and an honest face. The youth-group outreach projects await." At this point, Steve Lamacq's sadly missed BBC Radio 1 *Evening Session* was at its prime and he played the lead track heavily. The single even pierced the official charts, albeit at a lowly number 92, but this was a very good progression for only their second ever studio session. ('Brothers And Sisters' later appeared on the so-called *The Dead Cheap Fierce Panda* sampler and also as the B-side for future single 'Trouble')

Unbeknown to Coldplay, one A&R man was already on their trail, a copy of *The Safety EP* having landed on his desk months after its initial release. Dan Keeling was a recently appointed talent scout for Parlophone, part of the EMI group that also releases Radiohead, Blur, The Beatles, Kylie and Geri Halliwell. Suitably curious, Keeling had gone to see the band play a pre-Christmas 1998 gig at Cairo Jack's, an Egyptian-themed pub just off Regent's Street in the West End of London. The venue was small, the crowd even smaller. "I wasn't really that enamoured," says Keeling. "I thought Chris had something. He was quite charismatic. But the sound wasn't there."

By the time Keeling heard the 'Brothers And Sisters' single, he was already considering making an offer to the band. His interest was shared by that of Caroline Ellery at BMG Music Publishing who was also alerted to the band by the début EP and who later signed them to a publishing contract.

With three members of Coldplay still at college, many in the record business viewed *The Safety EP* and the 'Brothers And Sisters' single as a temporary hobby by students on the verge of 'proper' careers. In a climate when record deals were becoming increasingly scarce, with the already exorbitant cost of launching a new band on the rise, any group who might not be unconditionally committed seemed a risk not worth taking.

Eventually, in the late spring of 1999, an undeterred Keeling made his move and contacted the band. He was particularly impressed with 'No More Keeping My Feet On The Ground': "It just overwhelmed me. I wanted to stay cool but I could only hold off calling (them) until Saturday morning. I met Phil, but Chris couldn't come because he was doing his exams." Once other labels had registered Parlophone's interest, something of a cheque book scrum ensued but Keeling triumphed and eventually signed the band for an eight-album deal.

Fortunately, the three members of Coldplay who were still studying came up trumps in their June 1999 final exams. Despite all the exciting musical distractions, Chris earned a first class degree, while both Jon and Will both scored 2:1s.

The actual signing of the record contract took place in the centre of London's Trafalgar Square, only a mile away from where The Sex Pistols posed with their A&M contract outside Buckingham Palace in 1977. The silliness continued when they signed their publishing deal on a rowing boat in the middle of the Serpentine in Hyde Park. "We only had enough money for fifteen minutes (on the boat) so we had to do it sharpish!" said Chris.

The euphoric mood quickly faded. With a début Parlophone release scheduled for early winter of 1999, Coldplay's own obligations and the expectations of the record company hit the band like a truck. They were sent to record an EP with

Beta Band producer Chris Allison, to be called *The Blue Room EP*, but found the reality of the experience very different from the glamorous ideal most aspiring bands imagine. They were rising early to get to the studio, taking the crowded London Underground in 90-degree heat to the grimy, crime-ridden Elephant And Castle. The discomfort of their commute alongside millions of other nine-to-fivers was exacerbated by a summer of train delays and industrial disputes.

On top of it all, when they got to the studio, the chemistry with Allison wasn't right. "(He) was pulling us in a certain direction and we were kind of pulling against it," said Chris. "Half pulling against it and half going, 'Well, at least he's got a sound!'"

The pressure of their freshly signed record deal and the fact that after all the dreaming they were now in a professional studio, funded by a major label who expected results, rapidly took its toll, and on Chris in particular. He openly admits that the ticking of the corporate clock ground him down very quickly and he lashed out at the band – and Will – in particular. As he recounted in Q magazine, "Things were going wrong in the studio and I told Will it was his fault. He'd be out of time once and I'd be telling him he was shit."

"I was so nervous of us fucking up our chance I'd become obsessed with whether we were a technically good band or not" CHRIS

Not surprisingly, Will wouldn't stand for this and walked out. It would be a full, anxious week before the situation was remedied and Coldplay were back in business: "And it was all my fault," admitted Chris. "I thought to myself, 'You fucking twat.' I was so nervous of us fucking up our chance I'd become obsessed with whether we were a technically good band or not. I apologised, but I felt I had to pay, so I got drunk."

Chris remains a non-smoker and non-drinker, so it was all the more peculiar that he decided to punish himself by getting blind drunk. Filling his previously alcohol-free body with lashings of beer, vodka and, oddly enough, Ribena, Chris's self-destruct ended in a paralytic and uncomfortable stupor. Guy was in his own flat when Chris began the bender and chose to go out with his girlfriend, returning to find Chris dribbling Ribena-laced vomit on the floor.

"He's not been drunk since," says Guy. "Chris brings quite enough spice to our lives without alcohol being involved. When his energy is up he's brilliant. Creatively he's great. But when the energy is down, it makes things tough. That was a horrible time which I could never go through again."

On reflection, this drunken conclusion to a tempestuous week was a defining watershed for the band. Suitably humbled, Chris vowed to tone down his rather puritanical control of Coldplay. It later came to light that 'band rules' included the protocol that anyone caught taking cocaine would face immediate dismissal. More importantly perhaps, Chris declared that from that moment on, the band was a democratic group of four equal parts. Wisely, Chris decided that all future songwriting credits would be split four ways as would all income, despite Chris writing all the words and creating many of the core song concepts. This was in line with the policy favoured by other masters of longevity, including R.E.M. and U2. In R.E.M. Michael Stipe writes all the words, as does Bono in U2, yet both share all monies equally with the other three members.

Industry insiders suggest this decision, which has surely been central to the founder members lasting over twenty years together, has personally cost Bono in excess of £30 million. The question is, would they have even got past their first few albums had he – or in Coldplay's case, Chris – been earning far more than his colleagues? Rock and roll is a volatile environment at the best of times, but when you add personal resentment over vastly differing incomes to the powder keg, the results are often terminal. In light of recent acrimonious legal battles, perhaps most notably between the various members of Spandau Ballet, Chris said, "Do I really want to spend two weeks in court some way down the line arguing with my closest mates about who wrote what?"

Admirable as this new approach was, the newly democratic Coldplay still had very little material completed. After two months in the studio, these deeply fractious recording sessions had yielded only three tracks: 'Don't Panic', 'See You Soon' and 'High Speed'. They vowed to co-produce everything from hereon. Even so, Dan Keeling was a worried man.

CHAPTER 3:

HARVEST FESTIVALS AND THE FEEDING OF THE 100,000

Coldplay gigged prolifically at this early stage of their career, with perhaps their most notable showing on the New Bands stage at the Glastonbury Festival in June of 1999. Organiser Michael Eavis once said of his legendary weekend event that, "I regarded the whole thing as a cross between a harvest festival and a pop festival." The festival in Worthy Farm, Pilton, Wiltshire had long since established itself as the greatest annual British outdoor music event of them all.

Although the early drug-addled, free loving, hippified image of the oft-troubled festival was a million miles from Coldplay's own personal outlook, Glastonbury's origins were actually far more in keeping with their simple approach to rock and roll. In the autumn of 1970, farmer Michael Eavis booked the very first festival on his land near Glastonbury entirely on his own with no prior knowledge of the music business. The Kinks headlined and were paid £500. In modern times, the same headline slot would cost him £500,000. At that first Glastonbury festival, Eavis handed out free milk and provided a large ox roast (which was hijacked by hungry Hells Angels). He still lost £1,500.

Over the ensuing years, the festival became the granddaddy of the British weekender, equally well known for its muddy fields, disgusting toilets and torrential rain as it is for top music. Though plagued in the latter years with problems over licences, over-crowding and safety issues, for aspiring and, indeed, high profile bands, a slot at Glastonbury remains a huge coup.

Few students can boast playing at Glastonbury Festival just weeks after their final exams but that is exactly what happened to Coldplay. Their appearance on the New Band stage saw them deliver a polished, albeit slightly apprehensive performance. Already there were whispers about the band's potential and thus they attracted their fair share of journalists in the crowd.

The performance brought one member of Coldplay full circle. In the early Nineties, Will got a job working at the festival. That year, one of the main attractions was the Godfather of Soul, James Brown. Running around in the production area, word went round that Brown was proving a difficult star to accommodate. In the crackly ear-pieces of the production staff, an exasperated voice fizzled over the airwaves detailing Brown's latest requirements: "James Brown is refusing to go onstage until he has 25 Tommy Hilfiger rucksacks and a silk carpet to stand on." Laughing to himself, Will was not to know at that point that several years later, he would be on the New Band's Stage at the same festival. And when they played their 1999 show, Coldplay, in turn, were not to know that within two years they would be headlining.

"I had to hold her cigarette while she went to the loo" CHRIS

The largely unproductive sessions with Chris Allison needed to be supplemented in order to flesh out their forthcoming *The Blue Room EP* on Parlophone. Further sessions were shared between Sync City Studios and Orinoco Studios, during July of 1999, with both 'Bigger Stronger' and 'Such A Rush' being added to the track-listing.

While recording the EP, Coldplay supported Welsh popsters Catatonia at The London Forum in Kentish Town. Lead singer Cerys Matthews was enjoying a spell as both a *bette noir* and home-grown darling of the music press, but her band were destined to spiral into an unseemly disintegration only a short few months later. For now, this support slot was an excellent opportunity for Coldplay, their biggest indoor gig to date. At this stage, Chris was still a little star-struck by it all, telling *Guitarist* that: "I had to hold her cigarette while she went to the loo!" The size of the venue and the scale of the production stuck in their minds: "That was incredible, it was huge," recalled Chris in *Select*. "It was one of our best gigs and we were amazed at the size of their rider. They had JD and tequila, it really gave us something to aspire to."

The Blue Room EP was a little grandiose perhaps, but nonetheless boded well for future records, suggesting a natural instinct for the epic. Both anthemic and yet folky, the five songs successfully mixed slithers of several styles. Most notable was the evolution of Chris' vocals, which were becoming stronger by the day.

It was released in November 1999 in a run of 5,000 copies. The stakes were getting gradually higher.

This more high profile release opened the band up to their first real taste of press criticism. *NME* continued to champion them, saying the EP "hinted at the band's potential for stadium-destined greatness with a wholly civilised and occasionally dramatic take on the Radiohead/Jeff Buckley melancholic acoustic method of mass seduction." However, universal acclaim was by no means theirs, with many detractors chiding them for being overblown and, most commonly of all, miserablists. This accusation was fiercely denied: "All our songs have very simple emotions," parried a defensive, albeit honest, Chris. "They're either very happy or very sad, but never miserable… Oh, all right, the last track, 'Such A Rush' is pretty damn depressing. But the rest aren't, I promise!"

Steve Lamacq's support was substantial enough, but when Jo Whiley joined in the campaign, momentum really started to gather. Whiley had originally teamed up with Lamacq on the *Evening Session* but her 'promotion' to a daytime show meant her profile was currently far higher. This nationwide coverage for *The Blue Room EP* was complemented by heavy rotation on London's alternative radio Xfm which, although it couldn't boast the listenership of Radio 1, was seen as a credible source of new music nonetheless.

This rising profile coincided perfectly with the band's first nationwide tour, co-headlining with Icelandic band Bellatrix. This set of dates, their first trip out on the road for more than a couple of weeks, was boosted by a show at Liverpool's Royal Court, supporting the then critics' faves Gomez and the excellent Guided By Voices. At this stage, their motivation and aims were charmingly pure: "It's exciting," said Chris. "You put that bit extra into playing for a crowd who don't know you and your music. We always try and make an impression. We just want to get our music across."

Having spent December back at home, the band opened 2000 with a slot on the blitzkrieg '*NME* Premier Tour' alongside Campag Velocet, Shack and Les Rhythmes Digitales. Fortunately, Chris' pre-tour predictions that they would be playing to empty venues proved far from accurate.

With the sponsorship of *NME*, the band was bound to enjoy great coverage. However, it was evident to most ticket-holders that the gulf between what Coldplay were playing each night and what the rest of the bill produced was vast. It was an important challenge for Coldplay, not least because this was the first time they had played a longer series of bigger venues and larger crowds.

Hard to imagine then, that at the start of the new Millennium Coldplay were visibly "over the moon" to be playing Newcastle University; by the end of that same year, just twelve short months later, they would be the proud owners of a multi-million selling début album and a tour schedule that would in future only be able to be accommodated by the world's biggest arenas and stadiums.

CHAPTER 4:

TURNING UP
THE HEAT

As yet, however, Coldplay had not even had a Top Forty hit. All that was about to change with their March, 2000, release of 'Shiver'. Unfortunately, just as with *The Blue Room EP*, the sessions for this release were far from easy. Dan Keeling later admitted to being very disappointed by the first demos that were sent up to him in London from the band's base at the Rockfield studios in south Wales. He was so concerned that the sublime energy of their previous releases was nowhere to be seen, he got straight in his car and headed off down the M4 to confront the band. He met with a predictably cold response. It was then that he first fully realised the extent of the renowned close-knit clique that the four band members maintain to this day. "They don't like people sticking their noses in," he said.

The band recorded 'Shiver' using an analogue desk, rather than the feted and fashionable hi-tech digital desks so commonplace in the modern studio. Both vocals and guitars were re-dubbed on more than one occasion in the search for perfection. Smaller parts of the three song release were also completed at Liverpool's Parr Street Studios. Notably, both for this song and 'For You', Chris' guitar was de-tuned to make some of the more complex chord sequences easier to achieve. One of the B-sides, 'For You', was recorded against the grain in just one night and under pressure for results. This duo of songs was complemented by an acoustic version of 'Careful Where You Stand'.

The lead song 'Shiver' was actually written two years prior to its eventual release. In a rare explanation of a song, Chris suggested he wrote the track while thinking about Natalie Imbruglia, a statement that he later vehemently denied. Closer inspection suggests that the ex-*Neighbours* starlet may have not been the inspiration; instead the fuel for Chris' muse appears more likely to have been the fact that he enjoyed little success with girlfriends throughout his teens and early twenties.

Chris admitted that the single was effectively something of a stalking song and comparisons have been made to Otis Lee Crenshaw's classic country number, 'Women Call It Stalking (It's Just Selective Walking)'. He wrote the track during a glum period when he felt he might never find the right partner, something "most blokes do". He finally revealed the song was about a specific girl and that he believes that the woman in question knows it is about her. He was painfully reluctant to reveal too much however. When promoting this single, he complained that he found it difficult, even pointless, to pontificate about the meaning of his songs: "I just find all this really funny. It's just a song. I've got nothing to say about these songs."

JEFF BUCKLEY

Inevitably, given the nature of the transcendent vocals and dark undercurrent to 'Shiver', comparisons to Jeff Buckley abounded. With refreshing honesty, Chris had no problem discussing this theory: "That song *is* a direct nod to Jeff Buckley. I certainly was listening to nothing but Jeff Buckley when we wrote that song… so, yeah, it's the most blatant rip-off song, but it's still a good song, and that's why we kept it. (But) he would have done it better!"

Buckley was not the only artist to whom Coldplay were repeatedly being compared. Already whispers of 'this year's Travis' were circulating and, perhaps more accurately, the band was coming under increasingly attack for being shameless Radiohead imitators. Although rather uncharitable, it is easy to see why.

The stinging guitar of a Coldplay chorus often contrasted sharply with the much softer moods of the verse, while controlled falsetto was complemented by full tilt vocals, a Chris Martin vocal trait used right from the very first beginnings of his interest in music. This was definitely a Coldplay song, not a Radiohead tribute, but this was a comparison that would simply not go away (and more of which later).

Whatever the inspiration behind the single, it was probably the first real sign that Coldplay had it in them to become the next great stadium band. The media agreed, with *NME* – who were fast becoming the band's champions - saying, "'Shiver' stamps out their ambitious intent and marks them out as future stars."

The single was also helpfully listed on *NME*'s 'Turn Ons' chart at number one for weeks. The single also enjoyed strong exposure on MTV and spots on several B-play lists at prominent radio stations.

To this day, 'Shiver' remains a live favourite, particularly when the crowd invariably attempt to follow Chris' trademark falsetto vocals, usually with ear-shettering results. It is in the live arena that the song's subtleties explode into a wonderful, anthemic, even devotional masterpiece.

Disappointingly, 'Shiver' rose no higher than number 35 in the UK singles charts, but this modest achievement was a relief to Parlophone, who were already anxious to simply get more product out after the numerous false starts in the recording studio. However, it is important to remember that at this stage in Coldplay's career, there had been no 'Yellow', there was no album and their touring experience was limited to shows at smaller scale venues or as part of a multiple bill. "When 'Shiver' entered the Top 40," admits Will, "it was a real buzz. It was a great surprise and a great thrill."

"This was our only ever hit single and it wasn't really much of a hit"

In May, Coldplay made their television debut on *Later... With Jools Holland*, performing 'Shiver' and a beautiful new song called 'Yellow' that made an immediate impact on the studio audience. The opening chart success of 'Shiver' was then complemented by yet more tour dates, playing alongside Terris and (briefly) Muse. The band openly praised both Muse and another support act, My Vitriol, reinforcing rumours that Coldplay were very 'nice'. (Some members of My Vitriol attended UCL at exactly the same time and in the same year as Coldplay.)

Then it was back on the road for their own headline jaunt, opening at the Leeds Cockpit. This set of dates was the band's first tour to actually make some money, not least because all but one of them were sold out. Despite this growing success, Coldplay's modesty was still very much in evidence. At a gig in Harlow, shortly after the singles chart debut, Chris announced 'Shiver' thus: "This was our only ever hit single and it wasn't really much of a hit." How wrong you can be. With the chart success of 'Shiver' under their belts, the band was in euphoric mood and so headed back to into the studio to continue work on their first long player. The band felt 'Shiver' was the perfect taster to the forthcoming début album: "The general theme of the album and the message we're trying to get across is one of optimism and determination and it's almost like a mirror of our situation; we're on the bottom rung of a very big ladder…"

Before the album could be released, Coldplay had much more to do – not least another relentless round of gigs. Most impressive of all was a second appearance at the Glastonbury Festival, in June 2000. This time around, the festival was being televised on Channel 4, so the pressure was on every band that was performing. The weekend was a particular triumph for Travis (more of which later). Originally Oasis had been pencilled in to headline Glastonbury but when that failed to happen, Travis stepped into the breach. It was poignant for Coldplay that a band with whom they would so often be compared was doing so well on the main stage.

As for their own performance, the normally humble Coldplay were moved to acknowledge their potential themselves. Despite their mid-afternoon slot and the fact they were on the second, not main stage, the crowd in the cavernous tent still exceeded 10,000 people. At one point during the set Chris moved to the mike and said, "Thanks for coming to see us... before we get really Bon Jovi-massive." He later justified this by saying, "It's 'cos everyone has a go at us for being all humble and everything, I thought it was about time we took the reins."

Noted journalist John Robinson was at the gig and simply said the band, "play one excellent song after another, effortlessly growing in stature. As 'Yellow' effortlessly captures the crowd's attention, the conclusion 'next year's Travis' is impossible not to reach." Coldplay were equally taken with the experience. "Glastonbury was the best day of the year for us," recounted Chris. "It was the best day of the year for me anyway, I love it."

After each Glastonbury Festival, Michael Eavis organises The Pilton Village Fête, an unadvertised annual gesture to appease local residents weary of the annual invasion of 150,000 mud-caked festival goers. Bands invited on to this one-night 'mini-Glastonbury' frequently go on to headline the main festival at a later date. When Coldplay were asked to play the fete they agreed immediately. Even though this was a 'small scale' show, the audience was still over 3,000 people.

After two earlier acts, a voice came through the PA saying, "The guitarist has been taken ill and Coldplay will not be able to perform... Do you want them to perform?" Then on bounded Chris, alone. In keeping with the stripped down nature of the show, Chris played the show alone, his first truly solo gig. Jon had been diagnosed with glandular fever and so couldn't make it.

Chris was noticeably nervous and muttered a few typically self-deprecating lines in the direction of the crowd: "If you want me to stay I'll stay, if you want me to go, I'll fuck off." Opening with 'Shiver', he quickly enthralled the crowd. In fact, this show was a fine example of just how versatile his vocals are. Across the eight song set, he performed countless acrobatics without ever falling into the fatal Christina Aguilera/Mariah Carey trap of tuneless self-indulgence. At moments when Jon would normally have pierced the tent's roof with his searing guitars, Chris belted out seemingly impossible falsettos; other times he sat back and let the crowd sing the chorus for him. The nervous tension that lay behind his opening quip faded within minutes and he was soon waltzing around the stage, truly in his element. Coldplay fanatics at the back of the tent who have followed the band since their early days still cite this as being possibly the best gig they had ever seen.

As if the Glasto triumph wasn't enough, the band repeated the performance at an absurdly early 3pm slot at Scotland's T In The Park. This was an unexpected bonus for Coldplay, who were extremely weary from touring Europe and had only arrived from the south of France the night before after a 24-hour bus journey. Their live set here won even more critical acclaim than the Glastonbury show.

The band said they actually enjoyed the day at T In The Park more, mainly because it was not as chaotic. "That was just mental. I'll never forget that," enthused a newly shaven-headed Chris. Neither will indie DJ Steve Lamacq who was spotted by one reporter reduced to tears by their set. After their set they played an impromptu game of five-a-side football with Embrace which ended in a draw, the last time that the latter band were to be on a par with Coldplay!

Another live highlight of 2000 was Coldplay's show at The Scala in Kings Cross, central London. Although they played only eight songs, the encore was the memorable – albeit rather odd – cover of the Bond theme, 'You Only Live Twice'. Throughout the set, Chris kept repeatedly thanking the crowd for coming, although most of the audience were delighted to see the band in such an intimate venue for perhaps the last time.

A brief flurry around Japan before a similarly received show on the MTV stage at V2000 further bolstered both the band's confidence and their rising profile (at this show Chris said, "The charts don't mean shit to us. But it does feel good to beat The Corrs.") This was also the first time Coldplay spotted a band banner and T-shirt in the crowd, something they all cite as a watershed moment.

With such a bandwagon of festival shows organised and with the exploding profile of the band rising ever higher, it came as a surprise to many that they did not play the double-header Leeds/Reading weekender. Coldplay had a typically banal yet endearing excuse – Chris' father has a cricket team which meets up once a year and as he had missed the event the previous year, he couldn't let his father down again.

CHAPTER 5:

YELLOW

Although 'Shiver' had given Coldplay their debut Top Forty single, 'Yellow' changed *everything*.

The track had its genesis one night at Rockfield. It was a beautiful evening with a panorama of stars easily visible. The members of the band were all outside, looking skywards and generally feeling inspired when the main melody sprang into Chris' head. It didn't seem serious at first, as he relayed the tune to the rest of the band in his worst Neil Young impersonation voice. "The song had the word 'stars' and that seemed like a word you should sing in a Neil Young voice."

It wasn't long before Chris had the tempo of the verse worked out, but rather like Paul McCartney using 'scrambled eggs' for the creation of 'Yesterday', he couldn't quite find the right words. He was certain the song needed one *specific* word for its concept and saw 'yellow' written down somewhere in the studio. The lyrics quickly evolved from there, and with Guy, Jon and Will falling enthusiastically into line, they recorded it through the night. They mixed it in New York, although Chris later felt that the vocals were too subdued, too quiet. He later called 'Yellow' a "Welsh song" in deference to the studio where it was conceived.

'Yellow' exemplifies so much of what has made Coldplay so popular. It has rare and delicate resonance and is shimmeringly beautiful. The opening acoustic guitar chords are mimicked by an electric strumming before plunging into the clanging lead guitar line (strongly reminiscent of Johnny Greenwood from Radiohead), then back into the acoustic verse. Each time the song slows to a stutter before plunging back into the lazy melodies of the verse, it reignites the listeners interest once more.

The luxurious warmth of the instrumentation is underpinned by an ultra-simple drum track, at times as forward in the mix as Chris' vocal, which alters very little throughout verse-to-chorus and contains only a bare minimum of cymbals plus the occasional open hi-hat; likewise the plodding, smooth and occasionally ascending bass. Add to that combination Chris' agile vocal, all wavering emotion, gentle falsetto and near spoken-word whispers (and admittedly at its most Jeff Buckley-esque). The Coldplay frontman is never acrobatic with his vocals for the sake of it. The resultant song is apparently simple, yet a deeply sophisticated classic.

Of course, with Coldplay nothing is ever as simple as it seems. Famed for their altered tunings, sitting down with a guitar and trying to copy Coldplay chords will leave you with but a dull, busker-like imitation. For example, it was apparent to most muso heads that Chris had detuned his top string to a Dsharp, but what was not so apparent was that he also detunes the fourth string down to B (to make it easier to get his fingers round playing the chords). Without such detuning, you can only emulate the sound closely, but never exactly.

> "'Yellow' refers to the mood of the band. Brightness and hope and devotion. It's quite concise - you don't have to expand on it. It strikes a chord" CHRIS

The characteristic 'jangle' of the propulsive guitars is a result of similar experimentation. By detuning as described, Chris was able to strum the guitar and leave the top strings ringing out, thus creating that unique, lush sound. This works for the acoustic opening guitar but is also used by Jon for his electric. But then, just when you think you have figured out his nuances, he changes it just a little later on in the song. Yet Jon plays his electric lead line through a conventionally-tuned six string. With his deft string-bending, and the clash with the detuned guitar, the resulting surging overdriven guitars moved many enthusiasts to cite classic Sonic Youth. It is exactly this sort of unconventional tuning mixed with radical yet subtle writing that separates Coldplay from the mass of guitar bands out there. Rock and roll they might not be, but bland there songs certainly aren't.

"'Yellow' refers to the mood of the band," explained the singer. "Brightness and hope and devotion. It's quite concise - you don't have to expand on it. It strikes a chord." The fact that stars do not burn yellow, and that many of the things in the song are not yellow either matters little. The references to swimming, bleeding himself dry and drawing a line under something are all metaphorical slants on the extent of his emotional devotion. The reference to drawing a line is a nod to Chris' habit of making lists, and particularly of underlining the most important things on that list. There is even mention of a song-within-a-song, written for the unobtainable object of his affections, a neat self-referential swipe also used by R.E.M. and Idlewild.

Most people actually misread the song as a happy tune with an upbeat theme, even though it was actually another somewhat haunting ode to unrequited love. Chris was single at the time of writing it. Hence the repeated use of the word 'yellow'. "This is a perfect example of (a word) that just sounded good… It just works. I tried not saying that word so much and it didn't sound good. It has a nice ring to it… I don't even like the colour yellow that much… but I was not thinking about the colour as much as something shining like gold."

As for the oddly articulated lyrical themes, he continued in *NME*: "That song is about devotion. That's just about somebody throwing themselves in front of a car for somebody else… if it was your wife or something, or your best mate, I'd do anything for them and they'd do anything for me… The lyrics just arrived. You've gotta have overstatement in your songs, haven't you? I'm sure Atomic Kitten don't really want you do it to them right now, but that's how it comes across."

The video for the single was conceived and produced entirely by the band. Initially, the original concept was for all four members to be walking along a beach, bathed in sunshine, keeping things simple and bright. However, the actual shoot fell on the same day as Will's mother's funeral, so Chris was alone when they rolled up to record the footage. This might go some way to explaining the genuinely sombre mood Chris seems to be in during this clip.

The weather was atrocious and the rain unrelenting. Ever the pragmatist, it was decided to record the footage in the minimum amount of time possible – twenty minutes – and go home for a warm bath. Thus was created the famous minimal footage of Chris walking on the sands, bracing himself against the wind and rain. It could not have been more fitting and MTV and the countless other music channels which had recently sprung up through the growth of digital TV, placed the clip on immediate heavy rotation.

This TV exposure for 'Yellow' was matched by a tidal wave of radio play, particularly at BBC Radio 1, where Lamacq again championed the single. For the first time, hard-to-please regional stations classed the track as completely radio-friendly and consequently started to pick up on Coldplay. Even the newly-revitalised BBC Radio 2 played the track repeatedly. This airplay continued for weeks, indeed months, after the track was released, eventually making 'Yellow' Y2K's most aired radio tune.

For once, *NME* – regularly derided for being wide of the mark in predicting success for also-rans – spotted a legend in the making. The undertone of their review for 'Yellow' suggested they had wanted to deliver a harsh, negative appraisal, but just couldn't: "Coldplay are the Sunday School kids brought in to provide a little heart-warming interdenominational harmony. It's amazing how they get away with this. There's something undeniably enchanting about them. Whatever moves 'Yellow' beyond the realm of drippy 'Thom–Buckley' pastiche, it's a true gift."

'Yellow' was released in June 2000, the same week the band played their first continental dates. They were in the Netherlands when they heard the stunning news that the song's midweek sales suggested it would go in the Top Ten. At that point, they all agreed that even if it slipped back into the Top Twenty it would still be a triumph, and either way a huge progression from the number 35 enjoyed by 'Shiver'. As it was, 'Yellow' enjoyed stronger sales in the second half of the week and finally charted at a lofty number 4.

That night they were actually playing a gig in Holland to a very small audience of people who had never heard of Coldplay. After the show, Phil Harvey walked in to the dressing room (such as it was) and told them the news. The band were shocked.

Coldplay were invited on to *Top of the Pops*, a traditional rite of passage for all bands hoping to prove to their doubting aunts and uncles that pop music was a worthwhile career. Better still, their dressing room was opposite that of Victoria Beckham and her England football captain husband David. Now Coldplay were a *proper* band. Indeed, a household name.

'Yellow' was not just the anthem of the summer in the UK. The song went around the world and almost overnight Coldplay were the band on the tips of everyone's tongues. "I think we got really super caught-up in how amazingly huge it was," recalls Jon, "and it was like, 'Wow, all these people are singing our song.'" Will remains perplexed as to the extent of the success of 'Yellow': "I don't know what it is about that song that made it so huge. If we knew what it was about that song that made it so popular, this next album would be the biggest-selling album of all time." Within six months of its original release, there was even a Chinese pop star covering the song.

As it was, 'Yellow' turned Coldplay into very serious contenders on the rock scene and in the process sold millions of copies worldwide. It also earned them a clutch of award nominations and actual trophies including: Q Awards 'Best Single'; second place in the *NME* 'Single Of The Year'; 'Single Of The Year' in *Select* magazine; 'Best Single' and 'Best Video' nominations at the Brit Awards; and *NME* Brat Awards 'Best Single'.

More importantly, the single was crucial in the public perception of Coldplay. If *The Joshua Tree* was U2's turning point, then 'Yellow' was a mini-version of the same for Coldplay. Now universally acknowledged as a classic ballad, the song has since gone on to receive some of the most generous plaudits. Fellow songwriters and artists were quick to heap praise on the track and Coldplay. Elton John said 'Yellow' was "the only song from the last five years that I wish I had written". Puff Daddy and Justin Timberlake were other stars who fell over themselves to praise the song. Liam Gallagher came backstage after a later Coldplay show at the Shepherd's Bush Empire in west London and told Chris that the song, "made him want to start writing songs again". He subsequently wrote 'Songbird', a tribute to his new wife and ex-All Saints star, Nicole Appleton, a single that later went Top Three. Liam even leant over to Chris and sang the song in his ear.

TRAVIS

For some 'Yellow' was proof positive that Coldplay were – as previously suggested - the new Travis. Not Radiohead or U2, but Travis. In 1999, the Scottish pop melodists had seemingly come from nowhere to claim all the honours, with a clutch of brilliant opening singles, peaking with the tender 'Driftwood' and the anthemic 'Why Does It Always Rain On Me?' Their frontman Fran Healy quickly became the alternative pin-up of choice, while their album, *The Man Who*, hit the top spot and sold multi-platinum. Relentless touring and close camaraderie were just two more examples of similarities between Coldplay and Travis, so it was clear why the 'new Travis' comments would not go away.

While such comparisons are entertaining over a drink and provide endless copy for magazines, they can in fact be very damaging to a band's career. Embrace was tagged as the next Oasis, but they never seemed able to climb out from under that suffocating tag. It has cost many bands dearly. For Coldplay, it was vital that the comparisons with Travis (and increasingly Radiohead), however flattering, were not allowed to spiral out of control. The only way to prevent this was to deliver songs that identified them as very much their own men.

One approach was to self-eulogise. At a show in Norwich several months after 'Yellow' charted, Chris introduced 'Yellow' like this: "In the Seventies, there was Queen's 'Bohemian Rhapsody', in the Eighties there was Duran Duran's 'Rio' and in the Nineties 'Runaway Train' by Soul Asylum. We're Coldplay and this is 'Yellow'." He later reflected on this and refused to back down, saying, "What I was trying to say there was that I do think it's a really important song, perhaps even a defining one."

More poignantly, however, such tongue-in-cheek comments were never going to be as important as their actual recorded output in putting these positive but ultimately unhelpful comparisons to rest. Fortunately, with the forthcoming début album set for a July 2000 release, Coldplay were about to silence all the doubters and detractors in one fell swoop.

CHAPTER 6:

ONE THOUSAND, TWO THOUSAND, THREE THOUSAND... CHECK... FIVE MILLION

Initially, Coldplay had intended to record their first album in a brief two week spell. This was highly idealistic of course, not least because it took no account whatsoever of their sometimes anal tendency to pursue perfectionism and their previous slow track record in the studio. As it turned out, the album was eventually recorded in bursts between tours and sporadic live dates between September 1999 and April/May 2000. Consequently, several studios were used, including the by-now familiar Rockfield, plus Parr Street in Liverpool and Matrix and Wessex Studios in London (apart from the mellow 'High Speed' which was recorded at Orinoco Studios with Chris Allison).

Coldplay admitted that at times the multitude of sessions were pretty awful. Weeks of smashing things, rowing and ego-driven strops might make people who regarded them as 'nice boys' think about this supposed genteel band somewhat differently, they suggested.

At the production helm was Ken Nelson, who had previously worked with Gomez and Badly Drawn Boy. He worked alongside Mark Phythain, who programmed the computers. The standard Coldplay set-up was complemented by a pair of Fender Twins and a Jaguar guitar for Jon (previously he had been a Telecaster diehard). Chris purchased an old Jazzmaster too, which Jon would often use, although the old faithful Telecaster still appears on the majority of the songs.

The material that was written fresh for the album followed the Coldplay routine of Chris bringing a melody or sequence of chords to the rest of the band, who then put their own stamp on it. "It's like a factory production line", explained Will. "It just moves on to the next stage and it's not over until all of us have done our bit. And all our bits have to be agreed on by everyone else." Despite being so obviously central to the band's success, Chris has never claimed to be a solo singer-songwriter and enjoys the musical tensions and debates that being in a band creates. He also distanced himself from the purely autobiographical school of writing, instead suggesting that, "songwriting is a mix of fiction and myth. Things are very romanticized. A song is like a film in that you can say anything you want. So there are parts that are based on truth and there are also parts that just sound good or feel good. It's a mixture of the two. It's all imagery. It's not strictly truth."

"If we've learned anything from how 'Yellow' did then it's that you can't predict anything."

The band found the pressure of delivering their first album quite suffocating and there were rumours of arguments and uncertainty creeping into the foursome. However, they eventually pulled through and completed the record a week before mixing began. "In terms of music," recalled Chris, "it was the hardest thing we've ever had to do, and in terms of friendship and our commitment. It was more a case of frustration…. the most important thing is that every song, we've really got a feeling into it. And that's the first priority."

They toyed with several names for the album, including *Don't Panic*, *Yellow* and *Help Is Round The Corner* before settling on *Parachutes*. Again there was a metaphorical reason, essentially that the thrust of the record was about how certain things in life can seem like they are destined to end in failure or tragedy, but that there was often a safety net, a parachute, which plucked you back from the brink. For the UK's supposed premier miserabilists, this was veritable optimism. The album cover – photographed by the band themselves – was a shot of the illuminated globe of planet Earth which they took on the road with them, usually seen perched atop Chris' keyboards or nearby on an amplifier.

When asked whether they expected high chart placing for the record, they were understandably reticent to commit: "If we've learned anything from how 'Yellow' did then it's that you can't predict anything."

In the weeks prior to the album's release, the band had an intense and exciting strategy of promotional work planned. Yet they were already counselling themselves in the event that the album was panned. In terms of the record itself, they remained calmly hopeful about its prospects: "We just set out to make an emotional, passionate record, with good songs obviously. We were pleased with it, but it's always hard when you've finished something like that, to know if it's any good or not."

The very least you can say about *Parachutes* is that it is "good". One of the finest and most understated début albums of recent times, the record instantly transformed Coldplay from "the new Travis" into a group who would soon

surpass the achievements of the Scottish outfit. Bearing in mind that the band were barely into their twenties, this was a record of rare accomplishment, subtlety and sophistication, displaying a maturity well beyond their years.

The album's new material is reinforced by their three EMI/Parlophone singles, 'Shiver', 'Yellow' and two tracks from *The Blue Room EP*, 'High Speed' and 'Don't Panic'. In all, only ten tracks, but this was sheer quality, not quantity. The opening track 'Don't Panic' was in many ways a perfect indication of what was to follow. A notably short song, it begins with Chris' soft acoustic strumming, followed shortly after by Jon's piercing guitar lines, segued with an imploring vocal. This was an opening song that immediately made you sit up and take notice. When taken in the context of the currently in vogue (and initially brilliant) nu-metal noise, this was a clear, refreshingly brief and charming statement of melancholic intent. The lyrical lead of living in a beautiful world again defies the accusations of miserabilism and sets the album off in the perfect manner.

Next up was the aforementioned Parlophone single 'Shiver', which raised the tempo somewhat, with its *OK Computer* drums and spidery guitars. This track typifies the simple sentiments of so much of *Parachutes*, often touching on themes and emotions that everyone experiences. Then it is straight into the album's most atmospheric track, the wistful and delightful 'Spies'. First debuted at the Reading Festival in 1999, this song's acoustic refrains are both foreboding and sumptuous,

while the lead guitar picks are contrasted nicely by the Larry Mullen Jr-esque falling drum lines, but this was no U2 pastiche. By now, the textures and depth of Chris' vocals were really settling into the listener's psyche and this is a clear stand-out track. His falsetto pitches against the rising momentum and building rhythm beautifully, a clashing mix of jagged guitars and simple vocal balladry. Then the band drop the dynamics right back down, refusing to head-rush for the obvious thunderous climax, instead winding the song down to just the gentle repeated vocal line over a feather-soft acoustic wash. (Bizarrely, this song was later banned by an overly censurous Chinese government for alleged "unacceptable political connotations".)

Refusing to up the tempo, the fourth track is the even softer 'Sparks'. Jeff Buckley and perhaps Nick Drake are the obvious reference points, but once more this is no mere tribute song. Chris' voice crumbles at times, before soaring into the gently controlled heights that he seems to be able to reach effortlessly.

Smack bang in the middle of the album is the clear masterpiece, 'Yellow'. Even if this had, as some feared, been the only decent track on the album, it would not have mattered. More than any other song, this will always be their signal of intent, a notice of ambition, their manifesto, their totem. With this single piece of music, they will always justifiably be held up as classic songwriters. Make no mistake, it is that good.

Future single 'Trouble' achieves the impossible and follows one of the greatest songs of modern times without appearing feeble by comparison. The soon-to-be world famous piano tinkerings at the song's opening confirm that here is a band unafraid to swim against the tide of fashion. When all around were using distorted guitars, on stage DJs and infinite Marshall stacks, here was a delicately crafted song that sounded quite exquisite, whether played solo by Chris at his piano or more emphatically by the entire band.

Again Chris using the lyrical trick of repetition, centring on the word trouble, although unlike 'Yellow' with more obvious reason. One of the few Coldplay songs that Chris has opened up about, he suggests 'Trouble' was the result of his own bad behaviour: "There were some bad things going on in our band... the song is about behaving badly towards somebody you really love and I was certainly doing that to some members of the band. I suppose it's about a time when I was being a bit of a knobhead." Of course, how he phrases that crude regret in musical terms is poignant, emotional and pure.

Once again the apparently minimalist sound belies the ingenious production process. The multiple snare rattles are mixed very low behind the desolate lead piano, so as to be almost inaudible by the time Jon's ringing guitars crash in. Yet there they are, keeping the momentum rolling, splicing each verse and chorus together seamlessly; a perfect example of "less is more". Critics might have started lambasting the softer emotional themes, the apologies, the unrequited love, the longing, but set against such a backdrop of gentle musical texture, this was hardly ever going to be an album for pretty hate machines.

The album's title track clocks in at just over forty seconds, somewhat disappointing when you hear the melody. Produced with a minimal of effects and unobtrusive ambience, the skin scraping up the guitar strings is not only audible, but actively part of the song. Why they chose to truncate such a promising tune to a virtual still-birth has never been explained, but it is a shame. Maybe it never evolved into a fuller song, or maybe this was the exact intention, to leave the listener craving more. Nonetheless, 'Parachutes' is the first sign on the album of the understated slipping towards being almost non-existent.

Weakest track on the album is the rather weedy 'High Speed'. Sounding like Travis at their wimpiest, the song never really takes off. Although Chris' vocals are compelling and the lyrics deftly arranged, the momentum doesn't quite work. Elements of the drums and bass sound recognisable but are actually rather just derivative of earlier tracks. Fortunately this track gains strength on stage but on the album, the dynamics seem too weak, promising potential but never fully evolving. It wasn't because this was the only track produced and mixed by Chris Allison either, the song was at fault. Hardly a poor track, for sure, but in such esteemed company, there was little room for error.

The penultimate track, 'We Never Change', kicks back the tempo and volume but returns the album to its lofty standards. Again opening with yet another acoustic refrain underneath Chris' accomplished voice, the song saunters along until Jon's piercing string-bending and almost Shadows-like solitary note-picking lifts the chorus into the stars. At first, the piano is barely touched, almost brushed across a few keys, while the bass simply follows the root note, without pretension but with great self-control (although elsewhere Guy's jazz influences are plain to hear). Even the rising climax contains fewer notes and less sound than most band's studio tune-ups. At times, Chris sounds almost as if he is falling asleep while singing, particularly on the final few lines which close the song, where a hint of laconic apathy seems to fit perfectly.

Ending on a typically obtuse note, 'Everything's Not Lost' clocks in as the longest song on the album at over seven minutes. One of Chris Martin's particular favourites, this song once more offers us piano tickles, guitar riffing of the most subtle and choosey kind, almost spoken-word vocals with fathoms of character and a masterful, polished production. Just like the opening 'Don't Panic' had hinted at the excellence to come, then so did this track remind us of what had passed and instantly urges us to press the 'Repeat' button. Just as you do, a hidden song catches up with you, offering a short, almost fairground waltz apology to a lover. Throughout the track, the drums remind the listener of the superb Flaming Lips, an airy, expansive rhythm backing that Chris admitted was a straight influence after having seen the Lips play a few months previously. Introspective. Wonderful.

Okay, many of the lyrics were largely incomprehensible. But hey, Thom Yorke had been hailed as a rock deity for singing about unborn chickens. And certainly Oasis was never going to trouble the Booker Prize judging panel. Chris deliberately steers clear of overtly political lyrics – at one stage Coldplay wrote a song that was a scathing attack on the tabloid media, but it was never recorded.

Of course, the influences and comparisons were obvious and multiple. U2, with many hints of the Edge's effects-laden guitar yet simplified infinitely; reminders of why Echo & The Bunnymen were one of the great bands (Jon made no secret of his love of Bunnymen guitarist Will Seargent); The Verve's Richard Ashcroft and for that matter their guitarist Nick McCabe; the late lamented Boo Radleys, particularly 'Lazarus'; of course Radiohead, almost at every turn glimpses of Yorke and Greenwood; The Flaming Lips; Kevin Shields' My Beautiful Valentine; elements of the languorous side of Pink Floyd that made *Dark Side Of The Moon* so appealing; Neil Young or was it Nick Drake?; the softer edge of Matt Bellamy's Muse even… and so on and so on.

Yet somehow none of this seemed to matter. While most great bands are often innovators, more still are accomplished magpies. With the quite remarkable atmospheres of *Parachutes*, the four former students successfully sucked up all their quite open influences and spewed out a delicate, enveloping warmth via a simply stunning album so ingeniously crafted and expertly delivered that only one band stuck in the mind at the end of the final closing note: Coldplay.

The context of *Parachutes'* release makes it all the more impressive. True, other bands had been tagged miserabilist, such as Doves, Muse, even Travis, but none had released a record like this. At the upper reaches of the commercial charts, the noisy behemoth of nu-metal, which had revitalised the tired metal genre and turned record books upside down in the rock-versus-metal debate, was sadly turning into self-parody, leaving Fred Durst enjoying increasingly less acclaim while suspiciously polished outfits like Linkin Park still sold vast amounts of records (their *Hybrid Theory* was the world's top selling album in 2001).

In the world of pop, reality shows were spewing up the occasional pearl among a morass of wannabe swine and the charts were filled with diluted trance, sugary pop and clichéd mainstream rap. Meanwhile, the all-conquering post-*OK Computer* Radiohead were about to veer off deeply into the experimental realms of the abrasive *Kid A*; Oasis were telling everyone who would listen that their *Be Here Now* album disappointed even them; Blur were heading for an unseemly part-split while the dance ubermeisters Prodigy remained on a lengthy sabbatical after their gruelling world tour for the ten million-selling *Fat Of The Land* album; hip hop was still struggling to pull its core genius away from the clichéd and repetitive; Stereophonics and Travis had sneaked into the gap to take the crown of British rock but here, suddenly, was a very serious new contender. In time, The Strokes would arrive and drastically shake up the music world, complemented by the eventual launch overground of UK garage, but for now Coldplay were head and shoulders above the competition.

Given this environment of predominantly nu-metal and pop, the fact that Coldplay had chosen to make their début in such a stripped back, naked style, that they were all only just out of their teens, and that they had been together for only 32 months made *Parachutes* an even more astounding achievement.

CHAPTER 7:

(UN)FITTER, BUT HAPPIER?

An intense period of promotion was planned for the days leading up to the release of *Parachutes*. Radio coverage was again substantial – Steve Lamacq's *Evening Session* continued its championing of the band by featuring some of the tracks. More prominently, the band played an in-store gig at the enormous HMV record store in London's Oxford Street. Over 700 fans, music press and Coldplay friends and associates crammed into the venue (there was a *very* limited amount of tickets on the door on the night) for a short, live performance featuring 'Spies', 'Don't Panic', 'Bigger', Stronger', 'Trouble', 'Yellow' and 'Everything's Not Lost', after which they signed copies of the album. The event was webcast and broadcast on Xfm.

"We do a lot of these but it was one of the best I've ever seen," Simon Winter, HMV's spokesman, told *NME*.com. "We were absolutely up to our limit capacity-wise, and I had to turn fans around outside. Almost everybody there last night bought a copy of the album and sales today indicate they could be number one by a long shot."

Winter was not wrong. The combination of anticipation, the sheer quality of the record and clever promotion meant that on the Monday of release, over 20,000 people were moved to go out and buy it. By the end of the week another 40,000 copies had been shifted, easily sending *Parachutes* to the top of the album charts. Dan Keeling at Parlophone had set a *total* sales target of 40,000, a figure that reflected the relatively modest investment in modern record deal terms.

These sales were moderately impressive, albeit way short of the hundreds of thousands often sold by the world's top acts. Oasis and Radiohead at their peak would have sold several hundred thousand copies in their first week. Coldplay, however, had legs and over the coming months the record hovered in or around the edges of the Top Ten until Christmas. In the process sales in the UK rose to more than 1.6 million, in other words, in excess of *five times platinum*.

There were several reasons why *Parachutes* enjoyed such longevity and accelerating sales. Firstly, the media almost universally hailed the record as a masterpiece. Few bands could dream of reviews like these. *NME*: "(Chris) has poured every thought, every feeling he's had in the last two years into this record… it's like reading one long, intimate love letter. Some moments here indicate there's more to him than anyone knows. 9/10"; Q magazine: "You can only wonder what well of emotional trauma has been dredged for some of what's on offer here. Halls of residence will echo with this record for months to come, but the rest of the world could do worse than listen. 4/5"; *Uncut*: "A sensational opening gambit and one that more than justifies the plaudits heaped upon them by the weekly music press. A wonderful record, very special indeed. 4/5"; Melody *Maker*: "Album of the Year! It's a fucking masterpiece!" and "very likely a defining musical statement of 2000."

"Shit, shit, shit. This is the weirdest thing that ever happened to us" CHRIS

It was actually difficult to find a bad review. Indeed, one of the few critical pieces written was actually a retrospective look at the album while reviewing Coldplay's follow-up record in 2002. It came from *The Guardian*'s Alexis Petridis who said *Parachutes* was "certainly no masterpiece. So timid it sounded like it was apologising for bothering you, its wan balladry was enough to make you wonder how rock music became so beige."

The second factor behind those colossal home sales was the success of the next single, 'Trouble', which went Top Ten. This reflected the band's higher profile, not least because the album with this song on was already out. Later, UK trance outfit Lost Witness remixed 'Trouble', a release that became an unlikely dance floor anthem. Initially, the plan was to release 'Don't Panic' from *Parachutes* but in the end the band decided that just the three singles was enough from that one record in the UK; in Europe 'Don't Panic' was put out as a single though.

Although three singles from an album was quite conservative by their peers' standards, when coupled with the seemingly endless airplay for previous singles, in particular 'Yellow', this ensured that Coldplay were rarely off the UK's airwaves, even when they were touring tirelessly abroad.

A third key element of the album's success was the string of awards it garnered, even though the absurd proliferation of modern day rock and pop award ceremonies has served only to dilute the impact and importance of many of these prizes. Nonetheless, despite the rather clichéd insistence of so many bands – most famously The Gorillaz – that awards are totally irrelevant, such ceremonies still matter. They are often televised and watched by non-committed music fans who rarely listen to the radio and probably buy less than 10 albums a year, and these consumers are invariably influenced by consistent exposure at awards ceremonies.

By the time *Parachutes* was heading towards the million mark in December, the media were already preparing copies of their end of year Best Of... listings. Thus the Coldplay album easily won the 'Best Album of 2000' plaudits handed out by *Select* and *Q* magazine, while they managed a slightly more disappointing Top Ten placing in *NME*'s list.

When *NME* chose its anti-establishment Brat Awards after the New Year, Coldplay came home winners again. More importantly, they were nominated for several Brit Awards, including Best British Group, Best Album, Best Single and Best Video for 'Yellow'. On winning the first two, Chris was clearly taken aback: "Shit, shit, shit. This is the weirdest thing that ever happened to us. All around us are bands we used to listen to when we were at school, sitting eating their tea. It's weird, and it's great. Thanks very much."

Later, when he returned to collect the Best Album gong, he recounted a time when he was supposed to be playing cricket at school but had also booked a gig that would prevent him from doing both. He said his teacher suggested that as he was useless at cricket he should play the show. "If we hadn't have done that,

I'd probably be playing for Essex or something now. Thank you to him for making us what we are."

By December of 2000 *Parachutes* did indeed pass the one million copies sold mark in the UK, only 960,000 more than the record company target.

The fourth factor in building these stunning sales figures – and the band's growing critical reputation – was their continued heavy touring. Just prior to the album's launch, they played a homecoming gig for Chris at Exeter's Cavern Club and the crowd reaction was an indication of what was about to happen to Coldplay in the coming months.

Chris was visibly thrilled to be playing Exeter and asked the audience to all say hello to his parents who were in attendance. "This is great! It's what you dream of at school!" Unfortunately, the *NME*'s Victoria Segal was less than impressed: "There's something undeniably irritating about a band who try quite so hard to be ordinary, who would rather offer up the drippy piano apologies of 'Trouble' than face up to a hammer-and-tongs fight, who tell the audience with such merry shrugging 'we haven't got all the answers', when the best bands have you believing they have a smudged copy of *The Book Of Life* under their beds." Segal was in a tiny minority if Coldplay ticket sales were anything to go by. That autumn, the band embarked on their first large-scale UK headlining tour, sold out within hours.

While the plaudits continued to pour in for Coldplay's album and live show, Chris was predictably more self-deprecating. He has even admitted that he impersonates Bono at home and ended up using elements of this mimicry on stage, particularly the heavy breathing and crackled vocals that the U2 man so

often delivers. Chris' notorious one-liners and ad-libbing in between songs has led to more comparisons with Thom Yorke, although Chris feels his conversational style is still littered with inappropriate comments: "Nine out of ten times I come off stage and say, 'That was a good gig, but I'm sorry for being such a knob.'" In Portsmouth for one show, the band had to agree, not least because Chris walked out and said, "Hello Plymouth!"

In among this legion of dates were several shows which proved central to the band's success. An acoustic-only gig – the band's first – at Ronnie Scott's in Birmingham on July 30 was an enjoyable precursor to a lengthy series of home dates. Though they had previously given unplugged radio performances of 'Yellow' and 'Shiver' in particular, this was the first full set before a demanding and musically educated audience too.

Complementing these smaller shows were some highly successful appearances at major festivals, most notably at the V2000 Festival in Chelmsford and Staffordshire. The larger shows blended with smaller scale shows and more private affairs: in August, they taped an afternoon set at the tiny Monarch pub in north London's Camden, recorded for the forthcoming TV series, *The Barfly Sessions*, which was to be aired on Channel 4.

Many of these smaller shows were already booked before *Parachutes* had been released, so the lucky few who booked tickets for gigs at venues such as Edinburgh Liquid Rooms and Portsmouth Pyramids could see a band that, next time around, would surely be playing huge arenas. The London date on this autumn 2000 UK tour was merely a single show at the Shepherd's Bush Empire. Some sold out venues displayed signs saying disappointed fans were welcome to sit outside and listen to whatever they could make out.

Barely pausing for breath, Coldplay headed out to Europe, to Italy for two festivals (where they told native journalists who would listen how much they enjoyed playing on the same bill as Marlene Kuntz), before returning to the UK for a BBC session, then back out two days later for a show in Barcelona, then back to the UK for two more shows that week before flying out to Japan within four days for the Summer Sonic Festival, before a two week gap leading to first the Bizarre Festival in Cologne, Germany and straight home for V2000! With the road crew having barely finished packing up the gear, they had to reopen the flight-cases at a festival in Holland and at another in Belgium.

This lightning blitz across Europe mixed actual shows with heavy album promotion and a smattering of acoustic gigs, in-store signings and radio sessions. Prior to the album's release, Coldplay had played only about one hundred gigs in total, so such an extensive international campaign was quite a culture shock. Within five weeks they pretty much travelled to most corners of western Europe, cramming dozens of interviews into each day before playing a show most nights. As if in an effort to clock up air miles, in among this continental trek were three dates in the southern hemisphere, at Auckland, Melbourne and Sydney.

After a superb 'secret' show at the tiny Kentish Town Bull and Gate, Coldplay's own Christmas celebration at the end of an incredible year, they enjoyed a few precious days off before the treadmill started all over again. The relentless pace picked up with another day-long flight to New Zealand and Australia for dates around that subcontinent before flying across the Pacific to begin a north American campaign.

Ideally, they would have wanted the promo tours for *Parachutes* to be over by Christmas. In reality they were only just starting. On the surface, Coldplay were coping well but the high energy performances gave no hint of the cracks that were emerging.

CHAPTER 8:

BED WETTERS, PLAIN AND SIMPLE

With the press files spilling over with gushing reviews and the award cabinets sagging under the weight of the gongs they'd captured, it is fair to say that Coldplay had enjoyed almost universal acclaim. Almost. There were detractors and, unfortunately for the band, this included Alan McGee, one of the music industry's biggest players. Owner of Creation records, McGee signed Oasis and boasted an independent label roster that included the Mancunian brothers, Primal Scream, Teenage Fanclub and a host of other critically revered acts. So it is fair to say his opinions about music were worth listening to.

The stage for McGee to voice his distaste for Coldplay's music was the Mercury Music Prize nominations for 2000. With a history of surprising and often left-field winners, the prize of £25,000 and critical nods was nonetheless much sought after. Coldplay were installed as 3/1 favourites to win, ahead of other nominees including Richard Ashcroft, Leftfield, Death In Vegas, Doves, Badly Drawn Boy and Nitin Sawhney. As it turned out, the winner was 10/1 outsider by Badly Drawn Boy, entitled *The Hour Of Bewilderbeast*.

McGee's problem was that he was disgusted at the list of nominees, especially since *Parachutes* had been short-listed when his own act, Primal Scream, hadn't. McGee had always championed his acts passionately but it was the manner in which he chose to articulate his displeasure that took many by surprise.

In a very public display of sour grapes, McGee vented his fury in a lengthy and cruelly direct article in *The Guardian*, deriding Coldplay as "wimps" and "music for bedwetters". Indeed, McGee's dislike of Coldplay bordered on the deranged.

Only a month later, McGee added fuel to the fire when he used an interview in *Melody Maker* to take another swipe at them. Talking about Kurt Cobain's widow, Courtney Love, he said, "She's about real punk rock, she's what it's all about, not like those twats in Coldplay. Coldplay are like something from an ice-cream advert, just complete careerists. They might as well be saying, 'Bend me over the desk and fuck me up the arse.' It's pathetic." So at least it was clear now that McGee wasn't a big fan.

NOEL & ALAN McGEE

This was sensational stuff for the music press, ever hungry for a headline. Readers either laughed, read into it that British music was dying, or just read it and move on. Others felt McGee was right to demand more rock and roll excess; opponents suggested McGee seemed to have hastily forgotten some of the output of his own label, such as the Eighties band Biff Bang Pow!, whose songs 'If You Don't Love Me Now You Never Ever Will' and 'Hug Me Honey'. Even his label's "critics' favourites", Teenage Fan Club, could hardly be said to be competing with Motley Crue for the title of the world's most outrageous band.

Others suggested that McGee, ever the opportunist, was cynically grabbing headlines to promote his own label. Creation had released the controversial new solo album by former Dexy's Midnight Runners frontman Kevin Rowland, which suffered a public mauling both for the music and the much-derided pseudo-transvestite imagery that Rowland displayed in his live shows. Rumours suggested that despite a substantial PR campaign from Creation, the Rowland album sold only a few hundred copies, leading many pundits to talk of it as one of the most badly reviewed albums ever released.

Also, to McGee's chagrin, the Oasis bubble appeared to be bursting. The Gallagher brothers had enjoyed a high profile and many column inches through their explosive personalities, but their current "rock stars in overblown mansions with expensive habits" routine had taken the edge off what had actually made them so appealing in the first place. Neil and Liam themselves were, of course, veterans of the band slanging match, having taken media insults to new heights with their relentless pillorying of Blur. By comparison, being called a bed wetter seemed almost a compliment.

Furthermore, although multi-platinum sales and fatherhood had evidently mellowed the Gallagher brothers, they were their usual quote-friendly-selves when they bumped into Chris backstage at a London show. Liam leant into his ear and said, "Don't worry 'bout fookin' McGee. We like ya. And if McGee doesn't like the new album then we really are shit."

Coldplay's reaction to this tirade from McGee was twofold. In the media, with the press sensing the first whiff of a genuine rock'n'roll spat for ages, they came out fighting. "(I don't) give a shit what he has to say. It doesn't matter," said an apparently scornful Chris, while Jon said, "We are trying to be who we are, but that's about it. Pretending to be 'a bit mad' would just be sad." Other verbal parries to the McGee thrust were reported to include, "Yes, but he just an old punk, isn't he?"; "Well, that doesn't concern us in the slightest. It's not even worth responding to, really."; "We don't hit people. I'm tempted to have a go at that bloke who used to run that label but I just can't be bothered. That whole thing about him – I forget his name…"; Jonny provided the most granny-baiting quote of all: "On balance, I'd take nice over being called a cunt any day."

"We're starting to feel that everyone's out to get us. The more people that like us, the more people seem to hate us" CHRIS

On a more serious note, what annoyed Coldplay most of all was that McGee's criticism was directed at them personally and the personal venom was not the result of any actual feud, since McGee and the band had never met. In typically diplomatic fashion, Coldplay also made placatory remarks about some of the bands on Creation, suggesting that a man who had signed Teenage Fan Club, Ride and Oasis had a right to an opinion and even went as far as to say that *Xterminator* (the Primal Scream album which had missed out on a Mercury Prize nomination which had so infuriated McGee in the first place), was a great record. So after their initial defensive reaction, they had reacted – publicly at least – to being accused of being too nice by being… nice.

Privately, however, the bitter attack made a deep impact. The success of *Parachutes* had surprised everyone and the band found themselves thrust headlong into a relentless machine of media and promotion. Matters were exacerbated by the fact that their profile in the UK rocketed at a time when they were actually promoting the same album in Europe, so they returned to find, almost without warning, a nation that was suddenly Coldplay crazy.

Cracks started to show. Chris in particular seemed to have taken the recent digs very personally and his uncertainty suggested he was having a difficult time coming to terms with the vitriol that can flow so freely around the music world. "We're starting to feel that everyone's out to get us," he told *Melody Maker*. "The more people that like us, the more people seem to hate us, and it's something nobody tells you how to deal with. A lot of people seem to take it really personally that we're doing well, and I hate that… We're not evil politicians trying to swindle the whole world."

Chris even went as far as to suggest that McGee was ultimately right and that their album did not deserve to win the Mercury Prize because, "it's for trailblazers and we're not trailblazers yet. We constantly see bands we think are better than us." His self-doubt appeared to be rampant.

Worse still, there were industry rumours that the spell in the firing line had caused the band to turn in on itself, with whispers of stress-related illness, possible splits and inter-band arguments. The ferocity of the criticism and the depth of the loyalty seemed to have shocked Chris. "People who don't like you talk about you like you're the Third Reich. People who do like you will really defend you. So (at the moment) it's a mixture of extreme excitement and extreme, er, panic."

> "I don't like feeling inferior to anyone…
> I don't wanna feel there's a guy out there
> who's better than me" CHRIS

With the continued success of *Parachutes* creating an ever-increasing spiral of commitments across the globe, it seemed there was a real possibility that Coldplay would implode, crushed by the weight of their own success. The Mercury Music Prize awards ceremony thus seemed like an almost unnecessary final lap after the contest that had been bubbling so fiercely in the media for weeks. Jon was ill and unable to attend so Coldplay performed 'Yellow' as a three-piece. There were no major incidents, no waving of anyone's Oxfam-besuited bottom at Michael Jackson. It all seemed rather superfluous. And besides, Badly Drawn Boy's album, *The Hour Of Bewilderbeast*, won the Mercury Prize anyway. In an acceptance speech which would have made Sid Vicious turn in his grave, Badly Drawn Boy paid generous tribute to Coldplay for being gracious losers and so supportive of his work despite losing out. Nice.

Some months later when the dust had begun to settle and Chris and the rest of the band were in a more philosophical mood, they had clearly managed to draw something positive from McGee's outburst. Chris unashamedly told *Q* magazine: "You know what? I would like to shake Alan McGee by the hand. Quite right of him to give us a kick up the arse. I say, 'Bring it on', because it makes me think, 'I'll show you'. I don't like feeling inferior to anyone… I don't wanna feel there's a guy out there who's better than me."

CHAPTER 9:

CAULIFLOWER-GATE

"It's hard work being a soddin' icon 24 hours a day."
Ian McCulloch

In the ocean of weirdness and contradiction that is the music world, still waters do indeed run deep. While the release of *Parachutes* and the subsequent critical adulation, multi-million sales and sold-out tours created the impression that Coldplay were a band on the crest of an incredible wave, underneath the surface things were very different indeed.

Much has been made of Coldplay's rather fragile mental state, and Chris Martin has made no secret of the fact that he often worried himself sick. More often than not, he keeeps his anxieties to himself, but there are times when his public behaviour and dialogue with the press offer concerned.

At the *NME*'s Brat Awards in February, 2001, industry insiders were perplexed by Chris' erratic behaviour and series of bizarre acceptance speeches. He was visibly nervous and eventually ended up running out of the venue in Shoreditch, east London before the end of the ceremony.

Coldplay had won three awards, but this seemed to settle Chris' nerves not one iota. The first award, for the Radio 1 '*Evening Session* Of The Year', went without a hitch but as he collected their second award, for 'Best New Artist', Chris made a passing reference to British soulster Craig David. In particular he mocked his hairstyle, likening it to a cauliflower. It was hardly one of rock's greatest slurs, but no sooner had the words escaped from his mouth than Chris was mortified at having uttered a slight against a man he didn't even know. While Craig David probably just laughed it off, Chris dwelt on it and became deeply upset with himself. As he collected the 'Best Single' award he apologised and shortly afterwards made a rapid exit from the venue, running towards Liverpool Street Station where his girlfriend later found him alone.

His explanation for this erratic behaviour served only to highlight his insecurities: "I got there and I was sat among Oasis, Radiohead and U2 and I felt like this little kid, I didn't know what I was doing. Then I had to get the awards and I was terrified… I keep thinking lots of people are out to get us, when they aren't. I get paranoid."

After the second award, when his demeanour had worsened, Chris had convinced himself that he had been "rude about Bono" and in deference to the Irish rocker for whom Chris has the utmost respect, he felt he had put himself in "some sort of nightmare". Yet his speeches contained no such comments and no bystanders overheard anything about Bono either. Even Chris himself was confused, not sure if he had actually said or imagined saying it, or whether it was all down to jetlag. "I wanted to say, 'We're doing well and we've got a new album on the way.' But it came out as this garbled nonsense. I hadn't eaten all day and I had some champagne, when I don't normally drink much. I drank it out of fear." Even the much-regretted Craig David remark was askew, with Chris admitting, "I don't know what that was about. I meant to say Brussels sprouts and it came out as cauliflower. Everything came out wrong."

"Chris was going through mad paranoia and everyone was fucking worried" WILL

There were other extenuating circumstances. Chris had fallen in love around the time of *Parachutes* but the relationship had not lasted, leaving him badly hurt. Other reports suggested Chris was concerned that his hair was falling out. He seemed to be in a constant state of self-doubt about whether people liked his band, and confessed to being mortified about how insignificant it all seemed when taken in the context of the world's wider problems.

More worryingly, he said that he often felt that the next day could be his last and that he sometimes went around saying goodbye to people, just in case. Will watched with growing unease: "Chris was going through mad paranoia and everyone was fucking worried."

No one was more worried than Chris Martin. He was worried about the rigours of touring so much; worried about not being able to write better material; worried about what people think about the band, about him, about their songs; worried that they might just have one hit album and then implode; worried about being worried.

Chris was not the only member of Coldplay to experience personal traumas during this period. For Will, matters were much, *much* worse. On the day the band completed *Parachutes*, his mother died. Yet, because he had a happy childhood and came from a secure family, this did not seem to merit any sympathy. This hit hard, of course. "I can't say I had a harsh childhood, but I've had a lot of things to deal with, especially in the last year. People say, 'You haven't suffered'. It's like, 'Fuck you, you don't know what I've been through.'"

Jon and Guy had problems of their own. Jon had contracted glandular fever and was bed-ridden for much of the promotional work for the album, and totally out of action for a month, missing the Mercury Music Prize ceremony altogether. Guy was also becoming paranoid and unsettled, talking with Chris about how he thought the album was a shambles. As a result Will had to do much of the media work alone. At one stage, Chris hadn't done a print interview for months. He'd always said that talking about their music seemed pointless, unnecessary to him. Creating it was all that mattered.

This was unrealistic. He was now part of a global corporate machine, which would constantly solicit media interest and process endless requests for interviews. This was a necessary evil for all rock stars, especially for those at the beginning of their careers, but it did not sit well with Chris or the band. "This is not what we got into a band to do," said Will. "We're not orators. That's why we play music. There's something inherent in the music that can't be said, something that exists outside of speech."

On top of it all, Chris had become preoccupied with the fact that their commitments had prevented him from writing any new material. By the end of their European tour in the summer of 2001 he hadn't written a new song in months. They were spent, emotionally, creatively and personally.

Ironically, it seemed that as *Parachutes* became more and more successful in all parts of the globe, so Coldplay's difficulties increased. Rumours quickly began circulating that they were not coping well. On the road, Jon was reading *Das Boot*, a novel about the gradual and horrific mental breakdown of a troop of German submariners; the band quickly dubbed their own tour bus Das Bus in sympathy.

Other reports had them announcing they would do no more interviews, "either because we won't have to – because we'll be so massive – or because we'll have been dropped". They regularly cited the "Crispian Mills syndrome" – referring to the lead singer of the ill-fated Kula Shaker, who enjoyed generally strong praise and reasonable commercial success until a throwaway comment about Hitler saw Mills pilloried in the press and his band's career effectively terminated.

"We were a student band being back-slapped by Sylvester Stallone. We thought, 'How the fuck did we get here?'" GUY

Some journalists felt Coldplay's attitude towards the media was simply too defensive. For a band that had suffered virtually no protracted bad press, certainly nothing on the level of personal attacks and scathing criticism that some bands suffer, certain comments did little to endear them to their (few) critics. An example, from Chris: "That's what hurts – when people criticise you and dismiss all your effort in just a couple of thoughtless lines. Every time I read something which attacks us, even if it's only a tiny little thing in an article not about us, it gets me there. It's upsetting, but it makes you more determined."

For many this was simply just a young bunch of former students griping about the troubles of fame. Worse still, they'd only done one album, a few tours, and some press campaigns. What about those rock veterans who'd been in the spotlight for decades, toured the world countless times and endured the white heat of the media in their private and business lives since their careers began? Were we expected to empathise with a band whose only problem could be said to be getting too many great reviews?

To his credit, Guy acknowledged how absurd their complaints might seem, telling Q magazine: "I hate bands that moan, but there was no learning curve. It was a vertical gradient. I can remember meeting Sylvester Stallone in LA because he wanted to use 'Trouble' on the sound track for his film. We said 'no', but we were a student band being back-slapped by Sylvester Stallone. We thought, 'How the fuck did we get here?'"

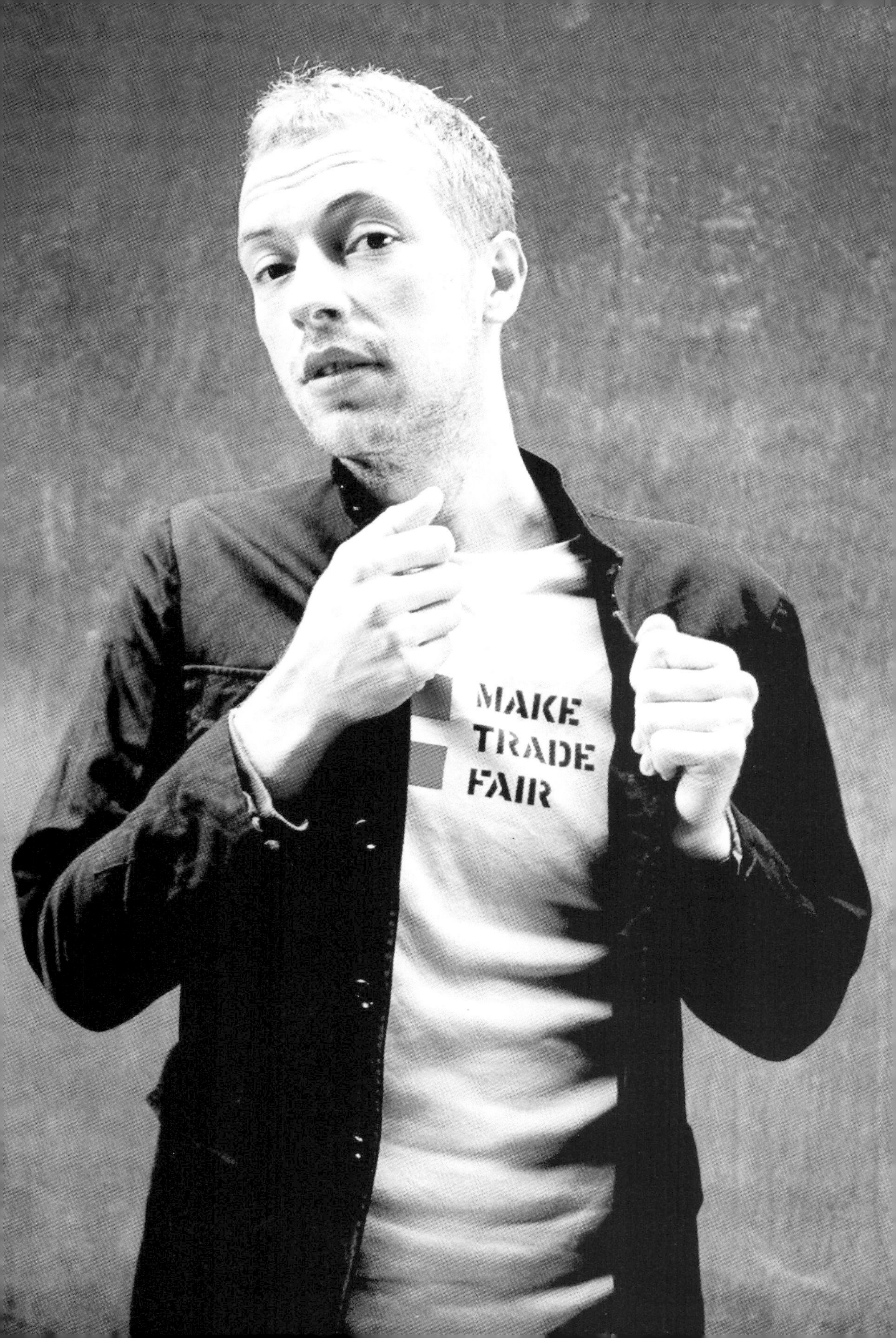
MAKE
TRADE
FAIR

Yet, some context is needed here. This is hardly a foursome of loopys, outcasts from *One Flew Over The Cuckoo's Nest*. They had only been a band for three years. Now they were being feted by all manner of celebrities. They had their self-doubts, but this was hardly a fault – indeed it is a refreshing change from the norm of bands playing the Bull & Gate in Kentish Town and announcing to the assembled 120 people that "we are the best band in the world!" That said, in typically self-effacing mood, Chris did manage to suggest they *might* be "one of the ten best bands in the world". Their work rate had been fairly extreme since signing to Parlophone. Will had lost his mom. Chris had had his heart broken. And let's not forget that before Coldplay's success they were students, whose sole purpose in life is not to work.

A further unwelcome aspect of life for Coldplay was adverse comment relating to their relatively privileged upbringings which, virtually since their inception, had been thrown at them as if to somehow invalidate their songs and their work. The band themselves were totally bored of the whole question and, to be fair, it was rather tiresome. The concept that poverty was essential to the making of a true artist, that it was necessary to suffer for your art, that a comfortable background was anathema to genuine creativity, was just a cliché, especially in rock and pop. Moreover, this promotes the ludicrous suggestion that, if you are jilted or a love is unrequited, provided you go to a good school or your dad drives a nice car, it doesn't hurt as much.

Change the record. For a start, this school of thought has little basis in fact. The long history of rock and pop offers countless examples of quite brilliant artists whose upbringings were far from destitute. John Lennon might have been abandoned by his parents and raised by an aunt but it was in the comfort of a nice middle-class, semi-detached home. Mick Jagger's dad was a PE teacher and his mum a cosmetics salesperson, so they were hardly dunking stale bread in water. Jim Morrison's dad was a well-to-do career naval officer. Pete Townshend's father was himself a successful professional musician while his mother kept an antique shop. Two of Pink Floyd came from very wealthy families while 'tortured genius' Syd Barrett, the son of a doctor, was decidedly middle-class. Genesis formed at Charterhouse public school. Nick Drake's father was in the

Foreign Service while Robert Plant's was an accountant. Bowie's dad was an administrator for Dr Barnados and Elton John was acutely middle-class. Even Bob Dylan, who famously attempted to blur the details of his background, was the son of a man who ran a successful electrical and furniture store. Moreover, much of the music business and the media that centres around it is populated by decidedly middle-class people.

It wasn't until the emergence of punk in the mid-Seventies that anyone gave much thought to the social backgrounds of rock and pop stars, by which time those who'd tasted success had adopted all the trappings of the middle and upper classes anyway. It was this distance between the stars and their fans that enraged the punks more than anything else and inspired them to vilify established bands as 'old farts'. The natural consequence of this class warfare was that questions about social backgrounds were now asked as a matter of routine, with deep suspicion falling on those would-be rockers from middle class homes. Thus did "difficult childhoods" and "council estate upbringing" become de rigeur for the architects of punk though there were notable exceptions, affluent backgrounds doing nothing whatsoever to dilute the impact of Joe Strummer and Hugh Cornwall.

Leapfrogging into the era of Coldplay, artists deemed not to have "suffered enough" often found themselves on the receiving end of caustic remarks that had absolutely nothing to do with their music. New Yorkers The Strokes, whose lead singer Julian Casablancas was the son of the millionaire founder of the Elite model agency, were constantly derided because of their privileged backgrounds. Julian and fellow Stroke Albert Hammond, the son of a successful songwriter, first met in Switzerland at the L'Institut Le Rosey, one of the world's oldest private schools, a haven for children of the world's super-rich.

This type of criticism is nonsense, and might even contain a trace of envy. The Strokes write about relationships, about emotional loss, about experiences which are valid for themselves and their fans regardless of their financial circumstances. This is not to suggest that those artists who have experienced a harrowing upbringing cannot draw something positive from it, just that it's not some mandatory requirement.

Nonetheless, Coldplay found that during the campaign to promoter their first few singles and debut album, they were constantly being asked the same question: are you just rich little college boys playing at rock stardom?

Of course, in typical Coldplay fashion, Chris Martin saw in this yet another reason to experience self-doubt, as he admitted to *The Observer*. "I'd think: 'Gosh, I'm just some public-school boy with my house colours. I've got a degree. I'm from a middle-class family in Devon. I've got no story. We're just a bunch of students. I don't drink, I don't take drugs, I don't smoke. I can't be compared with Liam Gallagher or The Sex Pistols, or anyone real. I haven't got any experiences as valid as the Wu Tang Clan.' I was incredibly insecure about it."

CHAPTER 10:

SPENDING TIME WITH UNCLE SAM (INC.)

Since the British invasion of the USA that followed the arrival of The Beatles in 1964, every British band with talent and ambition has seen America as a sort of Monte Cristo, Alexander Dumas' mythical island where Edmond Dantes discovered the vast horde of hidden treasure that transformed his life. It takes hard work to crack America, as well as talent, and those who do manage it can invariably be found occupying large country houses, not necessarily in the land of their birth. The late Sixties and early Seventies was the golden era for British bands in America but the post-punk pickings have been harder to snatch.

Though not strictly British, U2 managed it, as did Depeche Mode. Oasis didn't, at least not on the same scale, while Travis, Sterephonics and Blur sank without trace. Week after week sees the ever-optimistic *NME* hails a new band, British or otherwise, as having "cracked" the States or "taken America by storm". One such report had The Vines down as "invading" the USA because their album had gone in the *Billboard* charts at number 77. Meanwhile, N Sync and Eminem can shift more than two million albums in *one week*. That's cracking America. Thus it was that Coldplay turned their attentions to America. It might have seemed wishful-thinking on their part to hope to make an impact in the US only months after releasing *Parachutes* but its success had been so *total* in the UK that there were certainly grounds for cautious optimism. Indeed, small quantities of the album had already been imported into the US and sold strongly.

The process began by signing to Nettwerk Records (after some initial confusion), a subsidiary of EMI that was allied to an influential management company, home also to Avril Lavigne.

One of the Coldplay's first US engagements was at Los Angeles radio station KROQ's annual Christmas show, where they played on a revolving stage in front of about 8,000 fans. Suitably inspired, they spent the rest of the week in LA, including dinner engagements with Moby and Thora Birch. The real tour to promote the album was due to commence in the spring of 2001, with this trip a brief taster of the work that was to come.

The first US single was 'Yellow', which came out Stateside in November and soon attracted heavy radio play. US record buyers rarely embrace a band that has not conquered American radio, so this was a good start. In 2002 the most popular genre of radio in America was country and western but the normally conservative stations took to the Coldplay sound straight away.

The album was released just after 'Yellow', while the band was still busy promoting the record in the UK and Europe. The US media was impressed, though they were not quite as fawning as the UK press had been. Nonetheless, MTV declared that Coldplay's "sublime pleasures tend to creep up on listeners. Martin's cheeriness lends levity to the British quartet's set (with its) ethereal sound." Amazon.com called it "a wonderfully assured debut." Unfortunately, it was not until February in the New Year that they were finally able to start touring America and capitalise on this momentum.

Once again, 'Yellow' had proved pivotal and they knew it: "We've done practically nothing in terms of playing live there," said Guy. "The radio stations just went mad for it ('Yellow'). We're lucky to miss that initial treadmill of playing the toilet circuit." To their immense credit, Travis had already toured heavily around the USA to promote their *The Man Who* album and actually took copies of 'Yellow' to radio stations, telling them of the song's success in the UK. Although the Scottish band enjoyed some popularity, particularly on the student circuit, they certainly did not crack America. When Coldplay later arrived in the US to begin their own campaign, they found countless doors already open due to Travis' generous support.

Coldplay thus leapfrogged the lesser circuits and found themselves playing venues such as The Filimore in San Francisco and Irving Plaza in New York. In turn, this gave the impression that they were much bigger Stateside than their modest sales suggested. One benefit was that their hotels on the road varied from modest to luxurious, as against the $20-a-night hovels that so many Brit bands have to endure on their early US tours. Chris still took exception to American TV, in particular the adverts, and found the whole culture fascinating yet revolting. Hopefully he will eventually turn this into grist for his mill, as so many writers have done before him.

They played a dozen north American dates in the spring of 2001 and then returned in late May for another sixteen shows, then seven more in December of that year, and sales of *Parachutes* in the US were boosted by yet another strong radio single, 'Shiver'. This was a solid start albeit far removed from the three years of solid touring that they had been led to believe would be required.

In mid-August, 2002, just prior to the release of their second album, Coldplay played arguably their most high profile US gig to date, at New York's famous Bowery Ballroom. They again faced a crowd of thousands, among who were the Gallagher brothers (and Gwyneth Paltrow). The first mention of Oasis came with a reference to Noel's recent car crash, Chris dedicating 'God Put A Smile On Your Face' to "anybody who's been in a car accident recently",

NOEL GALLAGHER WITH CHRIS ON STAGE

With the set apparently finished, Chris suggested anyone who wanted a few surprises might stay behind. He then returned and sat down at the piano to sing 'Songbird', written by Liam Gallagher for his wife Nicole Appleton, formerly of All Saints and now a member of Appleton with her sister Natalie. This tribute brought the relationship with Oasis full circle from that night way back when Liam told Chris that 'Yellow' had made him want to write songs again. Onlookers reported that Noel Gallagher jumped to his feet and cheered loudly when Chris struck up the opening chords of his brother's song. Chris then closed the show with another cover, this time Echo & The Bunnymen's 'Lips Like Sugar'.

A few days later, in Los Angeles, the star-studded crowds included both Jack Nicholson and Minnie Driver. Chris dedicated 'Everything's Not Lost' to "all the actors and actresses in the house" and even changed the lyrics to: "And if you haven't won an Oscar, and you think that all is lost." Other celebrity fans spotted at Coldplay gigs have included Sean Penn, Heather Graham, Puff Daddy, Justin Timberlake, Brad Pitt and Elton John.

With UK sales heading towards the two million mark, *Parachutes* US progress would almost double that within a few months. By the end of 2001, they had shifted 500,000, but by the summer of 2002 that had rocketed to 1.75 million copies in the US alone. Soon after, they won a prestigious Grammy for 'Best

Alternative Album'. All this, coupled with UK sales and the modest but positive quantities sold in other countries such as Japan and parts of Europe, meant that by by the time the band were ready to release their follow-up record, the debut album had managed a staggering 5.5 million copies. Remember that original target of 40,000? EMI must have been mildly pleased.

As America came increasingly under Coldplay's spell, their infamous insistence on controlling every aspect of everything to do with the band became more and more difficult to maintain. This fierce control manifests itself in many different ways. Coldplay took the photograph for the cover of their début album themselves; after their early studio difficulties they agreed, as mentioned, to co-produce every record; they are central to the design and artwork of every sleeve of every release; they take control of every video, from concept to direction; they never allow any Coldplay track to be used on advertisements or film soundtracks despite several extremely lucrative offers. In 2003, Chris said, "Now we've asked that we are not even informed of the offers anymore. We just turn them down straightaway. I know we could divert the money offered into worthwhile causes, but we'd be cheating the people who bought our records, wouldn't we?" It is said they have already turned down offers in excess of £4 million in offers from American soft drink manufacturers Gatorade (for 'Yellow') and Diet Coke (for 'Trouble').

Whether Coldplay can to maintain this control remains to be seen. Younger bands often make similarly strident statements, but soften later in their careers when capitalising on their assets seem like a comfortable option. The same applies to sponsorship of tours, which at one stage was seen as the epitome of the sell-out culture but is almost commonplace on the modern gig circuit. Certainly, it has backfired for some artists – when Moby allowed every track of his multi-platinum selling album *Play* to be used as advertising and/or soundtracks, there was a fiery backlash accusing him of blatant commercialisation.

"We have 100 per cent control over any aspect of whatever we do, and that's really important to who we are and the music we make" WILL

Yet, exercised with caution and in moderation, it is doubtful if licensing of material for outside use has any real effect on a band's status, other than financial. Film soundtracks are a similar case in point. Many major bands from U2 to Prodigy to Limp Bizkit and countless others have allowed their music to be used in movies without any negative impact on their credibility whatsoever. Since the days of Trent Reznor's remarkable soundtrack to Oliver Stone's controversial *Natural Born Killers*, the role of the soundtrack – and the band's that play a part in that – has been turned on its head.

While it's unlikely that Coldplay would 'do a Brian May' and write lyrics for Ford adverts, ("Look at this car, look how it shines for you, and everything you do, and it is all Ford") selective approval in cases where quality control is exercised seems to harm no one.

Nonetheless, at this stage in their careers, Coldplay remain adamant: "It's been all on our own terms," states Will. "We have 100 per cent control over any aspect of whatever we do, and that's really important to who we are and the music we make… We're not a band that can be pushed around, although we do have some amazing advisors."

coldplay NOBODY SAID IT WAS EASY

Interestingly, in March of 2003, the track 'Clocks' was being used on ITV to advertise a new drama called *William And Mary*. There were also snippets of Coldplay tracks used on the comedy drama *Cold Feet* and even on news bulletins. Whether this was the first sign that the band were less precious about the use of the material in the media or not remains to be seen.

Whatever their thoughts about exploiting their music for financial gain, Coldpay are happy to use their music to promote fair trade with impoverished third world countries and assist work with other charities such as The Future Forest and Amnesty International. Tellingly, they refused to supply music to a coffee company that they believed exploited cheap third world labour.

While Coldplay have yet go to the lengths of more high profile rock campaigners like Bob Geldof or Bono, they feel an obligation to raise the profile of particular issues, to make people aware. "Our job isn't really to offer solutions," explains Chris, "as much as it is to advertise the whole issue. We're not trying to get on a pedestal, we're just using whatever media we can to interest people."

The most involved example of the band's commitment to Make Fair Trade was Chris Martin's visit to Haiti and the Dominican Republic in 2002. The tour of farming communities was sponsored and backed by Oxfam with the goal of persuading richer nations to alter their debilitating trade laws. This was no five star celebrity tour bus, no rider, no fawning fans and no press adulation. It was day after day of dirt tracks, malaria-infested jungle and exposure to destitute rural communities; not destitute as in struggling to make their social benefits last until next week - destitute as in "about to die". The trek took Chris to many villages whose residents have been severely economically (and by consequence in every aspect of their lives) deprived by unfair international trade laws. This means that the highly volatile coffee market, for example, which can fluctuate from one hour to the next in the hi-tech world of the twenty-first century stock market, can flip these people's lives on their heads without them even knowing.

The gruelling but insightful trip made a deep and disturbing impact. "It was like all the stuff I learned about in geography lessons wasn't just bullshit," he said. "It was real, all the deforestation and exploitation. It's going on and it's fucking horrific. When you see people whose lives are affected and you are responsible, it's like being kicked in the head." He also told a reporter from *The Sun*, "It was

amazing, unlike anything I've ever done before. We spent days in the back of
a pick-up truck, covered in dust. It made me feel grateful and even more driven
for us not to waste our opportunity. It was a big kick up the arse. I met this guy
who couldn't afford a guitar. He could be the next big thing and he hasn't had
any opportunity to do anything with his talent. I'm never going to take anything
for granted again." In photographs, on TV and at live shows, Chris has since
scribbled the words "Make Fair Trade" or that organisations web site address on
the back of his hand.

This is not a *cause celebre* for just Chris – the entire band is behind it.
"Anyone in our position has a certain responsibility," explained Guy. "Odd
though it may seem to us, a lot of people read what we're saying, see us on TV,
buy our records and read the sleeves, and that can be a great platform. You can
make people aware of issues. It isn't very much effort for us at all, but if it can
help people, then we want to do it."

Very early on in their careers, the band realised the rather ludicrous nature
of what they do for a living: "Of course it's rock star conscience," admitted Chris
to Q magazine. "I mean, I am loaded! And I love my life! And I'm selfish. I flick
through *OK!* magazine and look at the pretty girls and I worry about my
reviews and, yes, it's a cosy, cocooned existence. But I've woken up to the shit
underneath. When you realise that there are rules keeping people in poverty
because they're not allowed to trade, you wake up."

It was a natural progression from advertising the issues in their artwork
and interviews to actually performing in
support of the cause. Thus Coldplay readily
agreed to perform in Trafalgar Square in
central London for a charity concert
supporting Make Fair Trade. This brought the
band full circle really, because this was the
scene of where, as a completely unknown
band, they had signed their record deal to
Parlophone just four years earlier.

Another notable charity which the band
vehemently support is Water Aid. This cause
aims to provide safe and sanitised water in
some of the world's poorest countries. The
band even invited Water Aid to have stalls at
their shows. Oddly, the connection with
Coldplay was made when a librarian at South
West Water by the name of – Chris Martin –
spoke to Coldplay's singer about the charity.
The band have championed the cause ever
since.

CHAPTER 11:

THE YELLOW MAN

"People want their rock stars to pull up in a limousine. It is what they expect." **Freddy Mercury**

"Will is the nicest bloke in the world, but if you take his seat on the bus, then you've had it. This is as aggressive as we get." **Chris Martin**

So Coldplay had shifted over five million copies of their début album. They had started to infiltrate America. They were being talked of as the next great British rock band. But that wasn't enough. Not only were they apparently a bunch of lightweight school chums with no *real* life experience, said their critics, but perhaps most disturbingly of all, they didn't *rock and roll*.

They didn't appear to take drugs. Groupies seemed rather thin on the ground. Chris openly admitted to barely drinking at all. He didn't smoke either. Not one of them had had the decency to punch a photographer, head butt a fan or even cancel a gig due to "nervous exhaustion". Worse still, they got on with their parents, were glad they had been educated well and — most depressingly of all — they were generally "nice". They were certainly not the saviours of debauched rock and roll. What did this mean for the future of British music?

Oasis had reintroduced the outrage into rock and roll. While the likes of Travis and Radiohead appeared utterly incapable, or indeed interested in, overstepping the mark, the Gallagher brothers made it an art form. Countless fights among themselves, with photographers, bodyguards, swearing, profane gestures, inflammatory remarks, boozing, drug use, leggy blondes – they went for the full Monty.

Not so Coldplay. Their rougher edges were more softly sanded curves. They wore casual clothes, trainers, no outrageous haircuts, no tattoos saying "I hate Me" or genital piercings (as far as we know). They did start to think too much about their image in the aftermath of *Parachutes* but quickly realised the futility and transparency of that. They cited bands such as Kraftwerk, who were virtually unknowns on the street, as musical pioneers.

Their conservatism was not restricted to their appearance. Of course, this is not a quartet of Cliff Richards. Guy and Will smoke Marlboro (Lights). They all drink, albeit Chris sparsely. However, excessive nights out are few and far between. Chris didn't drink because he didn't like being out of control or the taste of alcohol.

Select magazine summed Coldplay up as "so non-toxic as to make Travis seem like darklords of hazchem vitriol". This was no *Hammer Of The Gods*, more an alcohol-free picnic in the park. This was one band who, if they did too much 'coke', would just get wind, where the only mainline they were involved in was the one that ran from London to the studio in Liverpool and for whom the word excess meant they had packed too many literary classics in their suitcase.

"I'd like to take Rachel Weisz to fly a kite on Hampstead Heath. That would be cosy" CHRIS

While Julio Iglesias boasts of bedding over 3,000 women and any rock band worth their salt dreams of dressing rooms crammed with scantily clad women, Chris offered this little gem about his own fantasies: "I'd like to take (Hollywood actress) Rachel Weisz to fly a kite on Hampstead Heath. That would be cosy."

Chris even admitted that in his college days he often liked nothing more than to go to the library and bury his head in the Bible. Although he is no longer the devout Christian that he was back then, he once apologised to his father in the audience for taking the Lord's name "in vain" after a fan pointed out that Mr Christian is an anagram of his name. Chris' faith, albeit diluted somewhat in recent times, was inherited from his devout mother who does not believe in sex before marriage, and he was clearly uncomfortable with the dichotomy of morals his career created. On the one hand, he was a young man in the band of the moment, so girls were always around. On the other, he remains convinced that casual sex always causes hurt for someone.

He didn't stop there, admitting to playing Scrabble on the tour bus with his girlfriend and killing spare time by jamming country and western songs. 'Yellow' he likened not to an orgasm or a drug high, but to "like a nice cake". When interviewed by one magazine and desperate to get out and about, Chris suggested (over two vanilla milkshakes) a visit to his fifteen-year-old brother's school sports day or, better still – and hold on to your hats – more kite-flying "I've got two good ones. It's terrific fun."

Sometimes the band didn't care about what people thought. "I like nothing more after a hard day's work," scoffed a sarcastic Chris during one interview, "than to do loads of coke, meet some local whores and slag off Alan McGee for half an hour. Before listening to Slipknot and swearing about how good Radiohead are, and how we should be more like them..." They even christened their approach "reverse rock and roll", saying that if the definition of rock and roll was "the seeking of the ultimate pleasure", then hanging out together and writing music was their nirvana.

At heart, and to their distinction, Coldplay never once pretended to be something they were not. Yet the odd thing is, what else did people expect? Three of them were graduates, the sort of people who make your heart sink when you see them at the local pub quiz, halves of shandies at the ready, all buoyant and knowing like a caricature of a team of *University Challenge* contestants. Here was a band that made their name playing introspective ballads and sophisticated, emotionally charged, melodic rock. "We are being rock stars," Chris continued. "We do it our way. I'm not going to take off my top and wear leather trousers. It's been done. We're not your classic rock stars by any means. We're not into mainlining crack or smoking our own blood."

Chris told *X Ray* magazine that, "I will lamp any idiot who says we're not rock and roll, because they're fucking idiots. I keep seeing, 'Oh, he's so boring, he just flies kites'. That's what I want to do! I fly kites and I go running! It's geeky but it's also what I want to do."

They do it for the music, man, which does sound incredibly earnest but at the same time is refreshingly honest. The extent to which they provide rock and roll's polar opposite is epitomised by the fact that when Chris was once asked what they had done that people might be interested in, he answered, "Will's a good swimmer."

The world tour for *Parachutes* seemed to go on forever. During the American dates in the spring of 2001, perhaps inevitably, Chris lost his voice. The highly anticipated New York gig (February 16, 2001) had to be cut short because of this and during a performance on *Late Nite With Conan O' Brian*, Chris was visibly uncomfortable (the cancelled US shows were rescheduled for late May 2001). They also pulled the plug on dates in Boston, Toronto and Miami. Later, a notice was placed on the official web site saying Chris was suffering from "voice exhaustion". Unfortunately, the American dates were not the only ones to be hit.

All of Coldplay's forthcoming European tour dates throughout April were cancelled. A specialist throat doctor who examined Chris warned that any more gigs at present could "result in total voice loss and could cause permanent damage". Matters were made worse by Guy catching the flu.

"That's the riddle, I think I'm crap, which drives me. But I also think we're brilliant" CHRIS

This was not the first time this had happened – a show in Edinburgh the previous autumn was cancelled for the same reason. Some claimed it was overwork, others that it was stress-related. This prompted Chris to taking technical singing lessons in order to strengthen his vocal chords (he started off by agreeing with the vocal teacher that he was "shit"). When the rescheduled dates were played, Chris repeatedly sprayed his throat with medicine, chuckling to himself on one occasion before telling the audience, "I should say this is cocaine, just to spice things up a bit."

It appeared, however, that Chris was experiencing another bout of lost confidence. He was mixing with mega-stars and selling millions of albums, yet still his personal demons caused him, to question his worthiness. He was clearly worried about being labelled as "that Yellow man".

In an interview with *Melody Maker* Chris' uncertainty was clear: "No, in a nutshell, it's not easy to deal with… It's just kind of scary, really. What's changed the most? Our state of mind. It's a very confusing time. I haven't been happy for ages." Fortunately, Jon sat him down and told him to stop the self-doubt, stop the apologies – often from the actual stage each night – and start enjoying himself. His comments hit the mark. "That's the riddle," says Martin. "I think I'm crap, which drives me. But I also think we're brilliant. Once we'd decided we had the chance of a lifetime we worked harder than we ever have in our lives."

Although they were at times exhausted on the road, playing live was the *modus operandi* for Coldplay. Talking to *Flavour.Lookon.Net* Chris said: "I hate all the rubbish food we eat when we're touring! But we absolutely love playing together, it's all we really care about. When the four of us play something together, something that we've made that nobody else can do, then I don't care how many hours I have to sit on a shitty tour bus or how many rubbish pasties I have to eat because when we get there and do the show it's great. It's why we're here, and I wouldn't change it for anything."

May 2001 saw the band kick off yet another sell-out UK tour. This was notable mostly for the fact Chris played an electric guitar on stage for the first time in years. As if to announce the move to a more aggressive instrument, he even threw his acoustic guitar into the crowd, causing an understandable scrum between genuine memento-seeking fans and people with their eyes on the prize of an e-Bay goldmine. Whereas before they had ended their shows with the Bond theme tune, later in 2001, they started concluding the set with Chris playing a solo cover of Burt Bacharach's classic 'What The World Needs Now Is Love' on the piano. Their own headline dates were supplemented by another appearance at the V Festival alongside such acts as a newly recharged Red Hot Chili Peppers and the unchallenging Texas. Their buoyant mood was boosted by the news they had been nominated for the prestigious 46th annual Ivor Novello Awards for the cumbersome-title of 'The Best Song Musically and Lyrically Award' for 'Trouble', pitching them against S Club 7 'Never Had A Dream Come True' and David Gray's 'Babylon'.

Fortunately, the band again managed to pull themselves back from the brink. It was probably a mixture of elements that helped them turn the corner. They became acclimatised to the media attention, while physically and mentally they grew accustomed to the rigours of the road. They realised that as long as they delivered what they considered to be quality music, there would be detractors who would struggle to pick away at their admittedly soft underbelly. And they started to become involved in issues beyond the often self-indulgent world of music, like the Make Fair Trade campaign. In difficult times, this could always deliver a short, sharp shock of reality.

Besides, they had their secret weapon up their sleeve. A song. One that was actually written at the very end of the sessions for *Parachutes* but had missed the deadline by a matter of days. They knew it was a classic, they knew this was the very hook which could pluck them out of their hole. That song was called 'In My Place'.

CHAPTER 12:

MAC THE KNIFE

Question: "Any tracks we should be looking out for?"
Chris Martin: "Nope. It's all rubbish."

Chris Martin belongs to the school of thought that believes songs are "given" to writers, that they are somehow floating around and the writer doesn't compose them so much as pluck them from the ether. He is thus not so much a composer as the channel through which the song finds its way to its audience. It's a concept shared with both Paul Simon and Keith Richards of The Rolling Stones, a belief that has its roots in historical philosophy, where competing academics have for years debated on the role of humans in the world, arguing for and against fatalism as opposed to self-determination. In this sense, and in its most extreme form, Chris' views go completely against everything else he says about his band, suggesting that he and the three other members of Coldplay are in fact no more than lucky bystanders in someone else's grander scheme.

Yet what about the work involved in getting a song out there? What about the production, the choice of instrumentation and so on. Clearly this cannot apply to the entire workings of the complicated machine that is a global rock band?

"When 'Yellow' arrived, I thought, 'Bloody hell. I can't believe we've got that song. That'll be a single.'" Chris claims that most of the words and all of the melody came to him at the same time, and that he had been "blessed" by this arrival.

Yet he also acknowledges that the band's personal decisions can hugely affect the final sound of that song. "Then it becomes exciting because then it starts to become Coldplay. Johnny starts putting riffs on it to make it better. That's what being in a band is all about. I'll come in with the start of a song and it's what everyone else puts on it that makes it a Coldplay song." Just as well, otherwise you could argue that all Coldplay did was place themselves in the right place at the right time to catch these classic songs. Blink too long and they might have fallen onto the lap of, say, Gareth Gates. Allegedly.

This goes some way to explain their decision at having pulled back from the brink of soft metal hell. Before their career had really taken off, they had experimented with some rockier, more metal sounds but thankfully they saw the error of their ways and diverted off into far more sophisticated territory. Having said that, Chris claims the only reason these fledgling efforts were never committed to tape was because "luckily, we weren't allowed in the studio then. Otherwise, we would have made a very bad version of *Back In Black*."

He continued, "It's a good day when you stop worrying about what people think you don't sound like and just worry about what you think you should sound like... there was a phase when we were thinking, 'Right, we'll show them.' We were butchering all these songs, but then eventually we decided we should do the songs in the way that they should be done and not just plug everything into twelve."

The subject matter of Coldplay songs is deeply intertwined with Chris' frame of mind. He has admitted he needs to be slightly morose, maudlin even to write well. He cannot see how he can write if he is in a serious and happily committed relationship. Much of this he credits to his father, whom he says is a terrible worrier.

Chris credits Will's willingness to put forward critical opinions as one of Coldplay's major strengths. Reciprocally, it is Chris' readiness to accept this criticism that allows their song ideas to develop as they do. Such candidness can lead to strife but as a general rule the band claim that sarcasm and insults are their favourite method of objecting to a particular track, lyric or sound.

Before finally starting work on the follow-up album to *Parachutes*, Coldplay had one enormo-gig in particular to play: supporting U2 at the 80,000 capacity Slane Castle on August 25. Chris had even invited the beautiful former child-model-turned-*Neighbours*-star-turned-pop-star-turned-cosmetics-model Natalie Imbruglia to the show on a date. Even more thrilling than this was the amazing moment when, halfway through U2's set, Bono segued a few bars of 'Yellow' into his own band's 'Bad'. Remarkably, after such a first-date bonanza, Natalie and Chris did not continue dating long-term.

Coldplay started work on their second album in October 2001, following a hectic twelve-month period promoting *Parachutes* which had seen them playing gigs every month since the previous October, many of them in the USA and Australasia. After the Slane Castle date, the band enjoyed a rare few weeks off before heading into the studio to start recording a follow-up to an album that had now sold five million copies. Chris openly admitted he hadn't written any new songs for months. At first, this scarcity of new ideas crippled the band. Chris even thought the band might be finished.

But all was not lost. At the very end of the last sessions, Chris was tinkering around on an old pump organ which a friend had leant to him. He was mimicking Jimmy Cliff and Procol Harum's 'Whiter Shade Of Pale' but the antiquated pedals and peculiar sound of the organ reminded him of drunken sailors, so he amused himself by trying to play a mock-sea shanty. The chords became the backbone of a new song, quickly christened 'In My Place'. It seemed magical, but since *Parachutes* had already been delivered to the mastering room this new song was filed away for future reference.

Two years later, desperate for new material, Coldplay dusted off and re-recorded this hang-over track from the first album to see if it got the ball rolling. What they captured on tape was, in their opinion, "the best thing we've ever written". Coldplay were back on track.

Within days they had a long list of songs in progress, including working titles such as 'A Ghost', 'Your Guess Is As Good As Mine', 'Deserter', 'Fingers Crossed', 'Amsterdam', 'Murder', 'This Hollow Frame', 'In My Place', 'Animals' and 'In Isolation'.

The production team was the same as for the previous album, with Ken Nelson co-producing with the band, alongside the computer programming skills of Mark Phythain. Progress was steady with the band attending the sessions with almost military discipline. Indeed, they felt like they were at a nine-to-five job, but nonetheless the progress was swift and smooth.

By Christmas the recordings were finished. The problem was, everyone was happy – except the band. With record company executives visibly breaking out into a sweat, the band decided not to release those sessions as they were and instead headed back to Liverpool's Parr Street studio, where much of *Parachutes* had been completed, to effectively start again. Eschewing the multi-personnel of a big London studio, just the elite six of the band, Ken and Mark entrenched themselves behind the desk and locked the door behind them. This intense gang-like mentality started working immediately.

Consequently, some songs, with titles such as 'Animals' (which had proved popular when previewed on tour), 'Idiot', 'I Ran Away' and 'Murder', were actually trashed altogether. "There was a feeling it was almost going too smoothly," explained Jon. "We were pleased with it, but then we took a step back and realised that it wasn't right. It would have been easy to say we'd done enough, to release an album to keep up the momentum, but we didn't. And I'm glad because now we have something we'll be happy to tour with for two years." A whole two years? What's this? Coldplay getting complacent?

Within two weeks, a batch of great new songs had been recorded, including 'Daylight', 'A Whisper' and 'The Scientist'. "We just felt completely inspired, and felt we could do anything we liked. We didn't have to do the acoustic thing, we didn't have to do a loud rock thing, we didn't have to react against anything."

"He's got it, I want to hate them but they're so good. He's too much of a perfectionist. He should relax" IAN McCULLOCH

While they were recording the new album, one very famous face was allowed into the inner confines of the otherwise sacrosanct studio – Ian McCulloch of Echo & The Bunnymen. Renowned for his outrageous self-belief and enormous presence, McCulloch remains to this day one of the most charismatic rock stars the UK has ever produced. At the height of the Bunnymen's fame, he was a genuine icon for the new age, and he is still held with great reverence and affection by many.

A Liverpudlian through and through, the band first met him in a bar next door to the Parr Street Studios. McCulloch shared a manger with Coldplay's producer Ken Nelson and after a few polite exchanges, when Chris nervously tried to buy him a bowl of soup, they eventually shared a drink and struck up an unlikely friendship. Within a few days, McCulloch was enrolled as a sort of unofficial consultant for the album.

Coldplay invited him into the studio and welcomed his suggestions about their developing material. It is there for all to see in some of the sounds on the record but it was perhaps the Ian's non-musical influence of which had the biggest effect on the young band. He was so seasoned, he had seen it all, been to the very top (albeit not in America) and, to an extent, slipped down again, and they drew great strength from his late night tales and seemingly bottomless pit of rock and roll pearls of wisdom.

Chris Martin was in his first year of primary school when Echo & The Bunnymen burst on to the worlds of UK rock with their epic swathes of pop and piercingly effective ballads. Twenty years later, Coldplay extracted from McCulloch the rare admission that they were the band "he would most like to be in today". "He's got it," said McCulloch of Chris. "I want to hate them but they're so good. He's too much of a perfectionist. He should relax. I never enjoyed that level of success and I think they should just try and enjoy it."

Their famous mentor did not just provide ideas and opinions on the material being recorded. For 'In My Place', Chris invited him into the singing booth to sit right next to him and even wore Macca's trademark heavy raincoat. Macca, who had been drinking red wine heavily, just sat listening and occasionally saying, "Go on, son. Go on."

Ian McCulloch oozed self-confidence, the one asset that Chris Martin so often lacked. Spending time with the Liverpudlian legend helped the Coldplay singer feel more assured about what he does, as he told *NME*.com: "I've met various people who've made me

IAN McCULLOCH

more and more at peace with what I do musically with my friends. Tim Wheeler, Danny McNamara and other people, but with Mac because he's so infamous and he's so as you expect when you meet him, all cigarettes and sunglasses, you're shit-scared for a bit, but then you realise that what's driving him is the same as what's driving you and your band." Observers commented that Chris somehow had a new swagger in his step that was not there before he met McCulloch.

Macca wasn't the only influence that came to bear on these sessions. The band had been listening to a much more varied array of music since *Parachutes* had taken them on that whirlwind tour of the world. German rockers Rammstein (who the band also befriended), PJ Harvey, Tom Waits, the hardcore At The Drive-In and the rather more obscure The Blind Boys of Alabama, plus older albums by The Cure and The Rolling Stones were all regulars on the Coldplay CD.

Of course, in typical Coldplay fashion, there were other key factors in keeping their muse primed and inspired for the new songs. Album opener 'Politik' was written on September 13, 2001, just two days after a pair of hijacked passenger jets slammed into the World Trade Centre twin towers in New York, in what was a very tangible realisation of modern Armageddon. By contrast, Chris' own personal relationships were still paramount in his thoughts when writing also. On a rather more comical note, his insecurities about his appearance kept bubbling up to the surface too, in particular Chris' fear of going bald. "But someone famous, someone who knows, told me Bono's had a hair transplant. Can you believe it? Bono? Some of those tufts have been stitched in. So there's hope for me yet."

Over the course of eight months, the album finally began to take shape. There were lengthy and heated debates about almost every aspect of every track, with the drum and bass patterns a special bone of contention. Their obsessive perfectionism often stifled progress, with rumours suggesting they actually used 1,000 hours of studio time for the eleven songs of the final cut. Yet more touring and Chris' Oxfam excursion also meant this was a lengthy and drawn out process.

"We're empty again now. Drained of ideas. Who knows if we'll do it again?" CHRIS

Chris was not about to let his anxious record company associates relax. With great excitement at the new album quickly leading to business talk of "the new U2" and multi-platinum sales four or five albums down the road, Chris was more than happy to put a spanner in the works, admitting, "We're empty again now. Drained of ideas. Who knows if we'll do it again?" Jon seemed even more doubtful of their longevity: "I honestly can't tell you where another (album) would come from."

Leaks occur in the rock world as much as do in Whitehall, and these self-doubts somehow escaped into the outside world, leading to rumours on the internet that the band were going to call it a day after the release of the new album. Much of the conjecture centred around quotes attributed to Chris on *NME*.com. Asked about the band's future he said: "As far as I'm concerned this will be the last one we ever make. But I hope that one day we have some more songs, you know? If someone said, 'You've got to start a new album tomorrow,' I'd say, 'I don't think we can do better than this'. We'll only do another album if we think it'll be better. I don't really care about the whole fifteen album thing. I like the whole Joy Division approach." He even suggested he might become a busker in London's Piccadilly Circus.

The gossip escalated when the original June 2002 release of the record, scheduled to coincide with a forthcoming Glastonbury headline slot, was delayed because the band wanted to spend more time mixing the finished tapes. Others suggested the band's decision to pre-release the track listing was another sign they were no longer interested in Coldplay – in the Napster-era, actual track names enabled fans to scour the internet trying to download tracks before an actual release. So many high profile acts had fell foul of this, most recently Oasis, who discovered to their dismay that all eleven tracks from their *Heathen Chemistry* album were already freely available to download over three months prior to the album release.

Such rumours were further fuelled by suggestions that Chris Martin wanted to quit while he was ahead and end the band on a high. His own familiar mumblings in the press about how he could die any minute because of the amount of flying the band were undertaking and how he always viewed every gig and song as their last, added to the confusion.

This was all nonsense of course. Notwithstanding the fact the band had a five album deal to honour, the rumours really were no more than that, web gossip. The band tried to dampen the gossip by explaining that without very careful mixing of the tracks the whole album could be ruined, a process that was taking them several weeks. This mixing was finally completed in New York, and in George Martin's Air Studios in London, before the album was pencilled in for an autumn 2002 release.

As if to confirm their current status as the UK's biggest rock act, Coldplay headlined their favourite festival, Glastonbury, on Friday, June 28. Just before that, however, they showcased samples for their forthcoming album at the Meltdown Festival at the London Royal Festival Hall in July, hosted this year by David Bowie who selected the acts to perform. Will even hinted that Bowie might appear on stage with them at one point. He talked of "a surprise guest appearance." Bowie didn't show, but someone else did.

The gig itself was outstanding in such an intimate venue but was perhaps most notable for the interloper who ran on stage during 'Yellow' and took over the vocals. At first the man's identity remained a mystery, which *NME* tried to solve by launching a tongue-

in-cheek manhunt for the shy new star. "Who was he - a budding star or a pissed-up twat?"

He was, in fact, Patrick Harvey, a 26-year-old from Birmingham who'd been drinking heavily all afternoon prior to the stage charge. When the band struck up the opening chords of 'Yellow', he joined the hundreds of fans who ran to the front of the stage. As he related to *NME*, "I thought 'I'll have a bit of that', but I went down the right side so I was on my own. I was feeling a bit left out so I thought 'Bollocks to it, I'm getting up on stage man!' I just bent my leg and up I was! I think someone came on stage to get me and Chris (Martin) waved him away."

Heartened by the Coldplay frontman's apparent welcome, Harvey plucked the microphone from Chris' hand and sang the remainder of 'Yellow' to fantastic applause. To make the day even better, he was congratulated by Natalie Imbruglia who was in the crowd. "I only did it for a bit of a giggle and never expected it to go as far as it did," he admitted later. Coldplay were unusually relaxed about the entire episode, especially considering that in former times this might have sent Chris into weeks of paranoia. Instead, they commented in the press that "Coldplay were not able to comment as to whether they would be offering Patrick a permanent position in the band."

The 100,000 sell-out Glastonbury headlining slot at the Pyramid Stage in June 2002 was unquestionably the highlight of Coldplay's career thus far, the perfect career-defining moment. Their work with Oxfam earlier in the year had made them even more motivated to play Eavis' festival again. "We've got to be good because now we've got more responsibility than just our own careers," said Chris. Thoughts of this prestigious gig had actually energised them while writing the new album, and the night itself offered a perfect opportunity to showcase some new material. Their fifteen song set, which included a three song encore, included a courageous six tracks off the forthcoming album. Strangely, the audience roared its appreciation at the opening notes of future second album-opener, 'Politik', even though, apart from the band and their close associates, no one else at that point had ever heard it before.

Chris was clearly overwhelmed by the event and told the crowd the band had been preparing for this gig for twenty-five years. To the great relief of many around Coldplay, Chris was in great spirits, even apologising for not being Rod

Stewart — the veteran rocker was due to play the festival later in the weekend. Indeed, Chris' nervous chatter appeared to endear the band to the crowd much more than the seasoned stage rapport of more established acts.

As it had been for Glastonbury headliners Radiohead, Pulp and even Robbie Williams before them, this show was the single moment when all of Coldplay's songs made sense, when tens of thousands of fans sang along to entire songs and when Chris, Will, Guy and Jon seemed almost lost for words amid the euphoria of the crowd. Most remarkably of all, the song that seemed to get the best reception of the night was the penultimate tune and future lead single of the forthcoming album, 'In My Place'. Chris later described the gig as "the most important day of our lives."

Just in case he might start believing his own myth, however, there was a shock waiting for him at the family residence: "After we had headlined Glastonbury and been pampered and told by everyone that we were great, I went back to my parents' house and got in trouble for not putting the milk away." Later, when his Dad picked up a copy of Q magazine with his son's face beaming out from the front cover, he said, "You must be pleased you got your teeth done, boy."

CHAPTER 13:

THE RUSH BEGINS

On first listen, Coldplay's second album, *A Rush Of Blood To The Head* lacked the immediacy of its predecessor. There were unprecedented changes of tempo, abruptly clashing chord sequences and far more understated melodies, often bordering on the bland. Or so it seemed. Like Radiohead's *OK Computer,* however, this was not a record that could be fully appreciated on first hearing. Only over time and with the benefit of repeated listening did it become apparent that Coldplay had comfortably surpassed their own not inconsiderable efforts on *Parachutes* and delivered a classic album of the modern era. Nothing else compares, indeed.

The juddering tempo of mournful album opener, 'Politik', was a clear sign that this new album was not going to be as easy a ride as its predecessor. Whereas *Parachutes* had seduced the listener from the outset with the gentle strumming of 'Don't Panic', 'Politik' crashed in with an almost-military, big-gun drum line, spliced with clanging guitars and overwhelming massed, sustained violins, the nearest thing to a wall of sound that Coldpay have thus far produced. Chris uses his acutely controlled falsetto to great effect as ever, in contrast to the hammering insistence of the musical backdrop. The usual Coldplay dynamics are present, though, a familiar reminder that this was the same band, with the characteristic drop from the pulsing thunder of the intro/chorus to trembling-vocal-and-chiming-piano-only verses. After two towering choruses, Jon's sparingly phrased guitar brushes on the bridge take the song onto an ever-escalating maelstrom that climaxes in what truly epic style. A shuddering, shocking and exquisite start.

Next up was 'In My Place', the track that may have saved Coldplay from an early grave and an obvious lead single from the album. When it was released in August 2002, it stalled at number two, kept off the top spot by *Pop Idol's* persistent king of cheese, Darius Danesh. However, the song announced loudly that Coldplay were back.

Without question Jon's finest guitar riff to date, reminding the listener of a cross between The Edge and the Bunnymen's Will Sargeant. Reassuringly cosy, it is one of the few songs on the record that can becomes familiar into after one listen. Opening with the hi-hat high in the mix, followed by the guitar riff, the track then falls back into the drum/bass/vocal and soft organ tones of the verse. The drums strain at the leash each tiome the chorus and *that* riff come round again.

After the more expansive lyrics of 'Politik', 'In My Place' brings Chris back to more familiar, bittersweet territory of regret and confessional melancholy. The mix of the anthemic and the infectious made for a potent opening single and must have had the record executives rubbing their hands together with glee. That this song was a throwback from the *Parachutes* sessions was demonstrably obvious, but it was done with such finesse that this mattered little. Had the band delivered an album worth of this material, which has such clear genealogical reference points in both 'Trouble' and 'Yellow', then they might have struggled to eclipse their first album. But as the next nine songs showed, this second album was very much more than just *Parachutes Mk II*.

The shadow of Ian McCulloch over the album sessions made its first clear mark on the third track, 'God Put A Smile Upon Your Face'. You could almost mistake Chris' vocal for that of the Ian, particularly on this song's enormous chorus. Even the lyrics, with their pseudo-religious references and epic flavour, could have been taken directly from the Bunnymen songbook. It seems likely, too, that Coldpay have been influenced by singer Stephen Jones, formerly of Babybird, one of the UK's most under-rated yet gifted writers.

'God Put A Smile…' was completed during the initial sessions before moving to Parr Street, but the band was not happy with the end result. Guy was concerned his bass line was too mechanical and inappropriate, so he and Chris sat down to work through and solve the problem. In the end, they wrote a new bass line, opting for a bouncy groove to fire the song along with an uplifting tempo. That was all it took and the song was now complete; prior to this, the track was going to be dropped from the record altogether – now it was one of the band's favourites. There's a whiff of the blues in the finished track though the vocal, for once, falls a little short of the usual high standard, not in delivery, but in the rather uninteresting melody. The closing bars reek of Ian McCulloch again, although there are also snippets of those other Liverpool bands, The La's and their later mutation, Cast.

Next up was another highlight, future second single 'The Scientist'. When this was written, Coldplay had about eight songs shaping up for the album in one form or another. Jon and Chris caught the train to Liverpool and reviewed the material completed so far, which led them to start messing about with an old, out-of-tune piano. Chris had been listening to 'All Things Must Pass' by George Harrison and liked the swirling chord sequence, so tried to replicate it whilst

mucking about on this piano. Suddenly the main chord sequence of
'The Scientist' presented itself and they both looked at each other, knowing they
had come across something special. They worked on it excitedly and it was
completed there and then, with the actual vocal and piano on the mastered track
identical to the one they created that day. Chris later recalled, in a brilliant
interview for *ShakenStir* internet magazine, how, "the best moment of the entire
record for me was when we came back to this song, that's my favourite bit on
the record. That was a great moment because it was brilliant."

Operning with one of Chris' by-now trademark piano lines, elegiac,
painfully sad and utterly hypnotising, the song plunges deep into Chris' fragile
inner world of relationships. His emotions are brought sharply into focus for this
track, with an unashamed and endearing honesty to his regretful, apologetic
lyrics, which rue the end of what remains an obviously deeply cherished love.
Yet another Coldplay song which could be as impressive with just a piano and
a voice, the gradual build-up of acoustic strumming, strings and clean, pragmatic
bass works perfectly. As with 'Yellow', this track displays a rare ability to present
a highly sophisticated song and idea in a form that seems almost child-like in
its simplicity.

As the second single from the new album, 'The Scientist' was complemented
by an awesome video shot between September 30 and October 3 in Surrey and

London, directed by Jamie Thraves, the man behind the videos for Goldie's 'Temper, Temper' and The Verve's 'Lucky Man'. Filmed entirely in reverse (in reference to the lyrics of "going back to the start"), Chris had to learn the whole song backwards. The disturbing clip shows Chris and his on-screen girlfriend in the immediate aftermath of a car crash, with her apparently lifeless body strewn across a field. Chris awakes from the impact still strapped into his seat, and as he runs away from the tragedy, it becomes apparent that his girl removed her seatbelt momentarily before the crash in order to take off her coat. At that split second, a lorry loses control in front of them, destroying them both, her physically and him emotionally.

Viewed alongside the neon brightness and day-glo world of MTV and the modern pop video, it is a deeply distressing clip, on a par with Radiohead's paean to suicide and rat-race self-loathing, 'No Surprises', with its devastating head-only single take video of Thom Yorke being gradually immersed in water (Thraves had worked with Radiohead too).

'Clocks', the third single from the album, hit number 9 in the singles chart in March, 2003; for the B-side, Ash's Tim Wheeler played guitar on '1.36' and Simon Pegg, the TV comedian, provided backing vocals on the same track. Another rushing piano line leads into a tumbling melody, which prefaces yet another stabbing drum track, although not quite as staccato as on 'Politik'. Curiously, this was the last track to make it on to the album, yet it seems impossible to imagine

the record without it. The credit for its inclusion must go to the 'fifth member' of the band, Phil Harvey (note how Harvey is listed in the liner notes for the second album with the rest of the band, not under management or the acknowledgements). He was convinced that the omission of the song was a mistake and insisted that the band look at it again. The problem was that the bare bones of the track were not working at this stage. Phil implored them to look at the music afresh and with great results: first the guitar chords, then the charging bass and finally the crashing drums suddenly fell together. The complex arrangement and accelerating climax are all handled with just the right amount of understatement. This is a fine example of the rest of the band knowing more about what to leave out than what to add, leaving the undoubted centrifuge that is Chris Martin to shine.

More chaotic and abrasive than the material on the previous album, 'Clocks' indicates that it is unwise to write-off Coldplay as mere balladeers. The hint of McCulloch lurking in the corner of the studio is undeniable, particularly 'The Cutter'-era Bunnymen, but this is definitely all Coldplay.

Yet more abrupt military-style drums abound on the oddity that is 'Daylight'. Mixing decidedly Eastern guitar motifs also reminiscent of 'The Cutter', with melancholy vocals and baritone backing vocals (surely courtesy of Macca?), this is a peculiar yet captivating number. Guy's bass is at its most agile although the uplifting chorus and falsetto vocal are a bit harsh on the ear.

The Eastern feel comes courtesy of a twelve-string guitar played with a slide, in a similar way to that which ex-Beatle George Harrison made all his own. The track was captured on tape very quickly, an approach which the otherwise perfectionist band positively pursued: 'We've been quite lucky," said Chris, "that we've recorded a lot of stuff down as soon as it's been written because you spend most of your life trying to recreate those first moments." In this way, the band played back a tape of the piano and vocal, played along to it and, subject to some clever loops and programming, that was that.

On first hearing, it seems as if the album is about to tail off, that the band's muse is spent, but fortunately they are confident enough to kick back from the sharpness of 'Daylight' and deliver a gentle, Lemonheads-esque 'Green Eyes'. For once a song about an apparently successful relationship, this jaunty tune features unadorned instrumentation, limited effects (save mainly for some vocal echo) and minimal backing. Said to be a direct result of Guy's growing love for country and western music, it reflects the band's growing confidence that they even saw fit to attempt such a chirpy number. Comically, Guy may have inspired the track but he was said to like the finished article least of all. This romantic track (along with album closer, 'Amsterdam') was recorded with the minimum of fuss and provides a perfect counterpoint to the epic likes of 'Clocks' and 'Politik'. A product of the original but largely aborted sessions, they returned to 'Green Eyes' four months later, mixed the tapes and it was done. Interestingly, the end of the song was written in Iceland, which Chris says is "the perfect place to write music."

The romantic flavour continues unabated with the openly sentimental 'Warning Sign'. Despite detailing a failed relationship and the part played in that by his mistakes, the feelings still obviously burn strongly and it is hard not to hope there is room for a reconciliation. For once, Chris makes no secret of the fact that this is a song of deep regret about the break-up with his girlfriend, 26-year-old radio executive Lily Sobhani, at the time of promoting *Parachutes*. They had been dating for a year, just before the band really started to take off, and Chris had even started thinking of buying a ring and proposing.

'Warning Sign' was an old song that Chris did not originally want on the album, but he was outvoted by the rest of the band who were insistent that its touching tones were included. Oddly, he says that the song makes the listener feel sorry for the singer when in fact he was, in his opinion, behaving like an idiot at the time. This mid-tempo, shuffling ballad is the result and here, rather than the guitars, it is Chris' yearning vocal line on the chorus which is the hook. Embellished with sumptuous strings and nursery school-percussion, this is a warm, charming song, reminiscent of Lloyd Cole. The false ending with sparse piano and soft strings appears to close the song, only for it to continue for nearly another minute and a half with Chris' increasingly wavering vocals and imploring lyrics. It captures the sense of unfinished emotional business that the lyrics describe.

A rare lapse comes next in the rather dull 'A Whisper'. Too overtly referential to the Bunnymen, this track is easily the album's weakest moment – the band later admitted that Macca had asked them if they had a song on the album that was 3/4 timing - they hadn't, so this was included. The vocal is too low in the mix, probably quite deliberately so, but nonetheless with the result that the top end just blurs it out, rather than sealing it as a whisper. The chiming guitars are too much a pastiche of early U2 circa *War/Boy* and the overall effect is disappointingly tame, rather like a derivative Sixties film soundtrack.

The penultimate track, the title track, with its haunting Pink Floyd-esque warblings, returns to more familiar territory (although it is hard to avoid the comparisons to Radiohead's 'Exit Music (From A Film)'). Sounding not unlike a western soundtrack, it is yet another ruthlessly simple song and production. Centring around impulsiveness, it seems to summarise the tone of the entire album. Again sounding like Stephen Jones at his finest, the vocals are almost spoken-word, until Chris screams into the chorus where Jon's stabbing guitar riffs accompany him back to the next gentle verse, at the beginning of which a slither of backing vocal from Chris sounds a lot like Bono. The country and western influence twang reappears with the string bending lead guitar, but the galloping drums and driving bass keep it firmly in rock territory.

The closing track is an atmospheric lament called 'Amsterdam' which in some ways reverts to type, but isn't a formulaic song by any means. The doleful piano and swooping vocals coalesce with refined precision, ably assisted by subtle backing harmonies, while the absence of excessive instrumentation lulls the listener into a becalmed sense of mellowness. Then, in a perfect example of the newly mature Coldplay, the song's entire solemnity is abruptly crushed beneath the weight of a crashing onslaught of sound. Like 'Green Eyes' before it, this song was a relatively easy one to write and was recorded pretty much live. Few bands can boast such dynamics, few think to try and even fewer can carry it off.

Overall, the album was a clear progression from *Parachutes,* yet the technology used was essentially the same. The bigger sound was doubtless necessary for the band to avoid the often problematic task of playing so many mellow songs on increasingly bigger live stages. Yet, it wasn't just a case of using more instruments and playing louder: they had all evolved immensely as players and soaked up many influences on their world travels.

Chris made the new album sound all the more enticing when he revealed to VH1 some of the personal events that had surrounded its writing (virtually all of which the band kept a closely guarded secret): "(It's) born from all the places we've been and the thing's we've experienced. Some of our friends have died and some of us have fallen in love. Some of us have fallen out of love and some of us have been to Haiti and some us been to Australia. Some of us have met Bono and some of us have met someone with nothing. It's like a massive culture gun fired at our heads. All this stuff has been happening to us, and now we have the opportunity to put it into some songs." That said, at a time when so much of music was obsessed with blending as many genres as possible into each album or even a single song, it was refreshing to hear something so focused, and so proudly ignorant of current fashion.

"A soulful, exhilarating journey, without once breaking its mesmerizing spell… the music is nearly flawless. This is exquisite stuff"

Coldplay had surpassed *Parachutes* and then some. What appeared at first as a possibly unwieldy and complex record was on further investigation a sophisticated, lush and elegantly produced masterpiece. Certainly the record by which all others of 2002 would be judged… at least. Chris had hinted that he was aiming to match his own favourite albums, particularly Radiohead's *The Bends* and U2's *The Unforgettable Fire*.

The fact that *A Rush Of Blood To The Head* was more of an acquired taste than *Parachutes* somehow added to the record's (and by association the band's) allure. The knowledge that they had found the recording experience so painstaking fuelled the feeling that this was a record of rare complexity. The tales of possible splits and personal arguments exaggerated the sense that this record needed to be savoured and enjoyed *just in case* those "final album" rumours proved to be true. Intentionally or not, the rumour mill swirling around the album had only enhanced its value. The only possible reservation was whether the more demanding atmosphere and depth would strike a chord with a public increasingly fed on a diet of reality TV pop and homogenised chart fodder?

The simple answer was a resounding no! In the UK, the new album easily took the number one slot on its release. First week sales were 250,000, nearly five times that of the first album. This was matched by a number one slot in many other countries around the world. Early sales figures suggested that the near-2,000,000 mark achieved in the UK by *Parachutes* was under serious threat.

America seemed ready to embrace Coldplay also, a very promising sign indeed – across the Atlantic, the album went in the *Billboard* charts at number 5.

What was very striking about *A Rush…* was the level of critical acclaim, which surpassed even the gushing reviews given to *Parachutes*. *The Guardian's* Alex Petridis wrote: "You feel you already know and like these songs the first time you hear them. The last band to pull off this remarkable feat was Oasis… it is all down to beautifully crafted songwriting and an all-pervading aura of warm inclusiveness"; *Amazon.com* praised "a soulful, exhilarating journey, without once breaking its mesmerizing spell… the music is nearly flawless. This is exquisite stuff,"

But for all his enthusiasm Petridis did have some complaints: "There is no mystery here. Whatever *A Rush of Blood To The Head* has to offer is apparent straight away. It is finely wrought and brilliantly realised, but devoid of charming idiosyncrasy. It is comfortable rather than challenging, varied without being devastatingly original."

"I can never listen to anything we do once it's finished because there's always something that isn't really finished" CHRIS

However, this was a rare voice of dissent. Almost universally, the album was received as a modern classic. All the band had to do now was tour the record to every territory that had bought into the project, which at that time looked pretty much like every record-buying country on earth.

Before setting off on a mammoth world trek, Chris had a few suitably unpredictable words to say about the record himself: "I can never listen to anything we do once it's finished because there's always something that isn't really finished… you just flick through the tracks, one by one by one, really quickly and it sounds like another album by another band of just eleven songs. And yet to us it's weeks, months, years of work."

Ahead of them was even more work. Parlophone installed them as its worldwide priority for 2002/3. This privileged position was helped by the fact that the parent company, EMI's other big acts – Kylie, Geri and Radiohead – did not have new records to promote. With the album in the charts, the critics in a lather and the full backing of the record company across the globe, stadium status for Coldplay seemed only a matter of time.

At the end of August, 2002, Coldplay returned to the UK after their lengthy spell overseas for a triumphant one-off homecoming gig at London's Kentish Town Forum, the same week that *A Rush…* was heading for number one in the

album charts. The last time the band would cram their by-now colossal following into a 2000 capacity venue prior to their forthcoming arena tour, the gig was one of the band's most special live shows to date.

The material on the new album demanded a more epic sound. For the older songs from the debut album, tracks like 'Yellow' and 'Trouble', as well as recent single 'In My Place', the devoted crowd sang the entire choruses (prompting Chris to shout "We've finally made it to stadium rock!"). In a self-mocking dig at their failure to beat *Pop Idol* comeback king Darius Danesh to the number one single spot with 'In My Place', Chris dedicated 'Trouble' to the lanky Scots pop oddity, saying, "Darius is more handsome!"

Introduced by Steve Lamacq as the show was being broadcast live on BBC Radio 1, the gig was a storming set. Again the crowd was crammed with celebrities, including Dave Grohl of Foo Fighters, The Cooper Temple Clause, Sean Hughes and Ash (Coldplay performed a cover of the latter's 'Shining Light'). They also played 'Flying Without Wings' by Westlife, a band they openly detested, plus a rendition of 'Happy Birthday' for manager Phil Harvey. All in all, it was a memorable night, probably more so for the band than for the ecstatic audience. Here they were, three years after their first gig, playing a rapturous 2,000 capacity as a 'small' show, having sold five million albums and returned triumphant from a fawning USA. "This is the most fun I've ever had in my life!" barked a delirious Chris Martin.

The international campaign got off to an inauspicious start when the band realised that many outside of the UK did not understand what the album's title phrase actually meant. Some Japanese journalists kept asking them if they were blushing with embarrassment at the record!

This was a minor hiccup in what proved to be an outstanding world tour for Coldplay. Before flying out to the US, Coldplay played an impromptu secret gig at north London's tiny Shepherd's Pub in Highgate. Not even a single employee at their record label Parlophone knew about it. Guy was absent with a cold, but the remaining trio still managed to work through a handful of their own songs plus some bizarre covers, including Bon Jovi's 'Livin' On A Prayer', 'Sweet Child O' Mine' by Guns N' Roses, The Sex Pistols' 'Pretty Vacant', T Rex's '20th Century Boy' as well as their usual rendition of Nancy Sinatra's Bond theme, 'You Only Live Twice'. After the set, Chris asked punters to donate money for Whittington Hospital, the birthplace of guitarist Jon Buckland. This raised £300. Despite these odd choices, the band's most peculiar cover has to be the one they played during a late 2002 tour of Europe, when they shocked their Copenhagen crowd by copying the bubblegum pop masterpiece/horror 'Barbie girl' by Scandinavia's Aqua. Chris took the role of Barbie and Jon played the part of her boyfriend, Ken. The cover only lasted one minute because the pair fell about laughing and could not continue.

Most impressively of all during this period was Coldplay's progress in America. With Nettwerk Records pushing the album for all its worth, they found their face on billboards all across the States as well as on hefty and exorbitantly expensive in-store merchandising and full page adverts in newspapers. Journalist Tracey Pepper from influential US music magazine *Spin* made no secret of the fact that the band were perfectly placed to take America by storm: "The music industry here is excited because they were one of the only non-rap/metal 'rock' bands to have a bona fide hit. Chris has become a truly engaging frontman. They're vastly improved live. They're also willing to put in the time touring. Breaking America is not a right. It takes a lot of work."

The initial three week push in the USA saw them playing in sizeable venues in key cities such as Chicago, New York and Los Angeles. Not for the first time did the band find themselves with many high profile celebrities in the audience but it was the frenetic nature of the audience's reaction that was so encouraging this time around.

"To my ears, they still don't have enough tunes to cut it live... after a while the tunes did seem to blend into each other"

The coming year would take them home for an arena-sized UK tour (supported by the magnificent Idlewild), back to America several times, numerous festival headline slots, Japan and provisionally Australasia too. The arena tour in the UK was final proof – if it was needed – that Coldplay were now one of their home country's biggest acts. The sell-out dates included two nights at Wembley Arena, which reputedly could have sold out five times over. The material from their two albums was complemented by occasional covers of the Bunnymen's 'Lips Like Sugar' and Bowie's 'Heroes'. Just what effect this daunting schedule will have on the various members of Coldplay remains to be seen, but for now, these were exciting times ahead.

Nevertheless, the live shows have attracted their share of bad reviews. Maybe it was the mellow nature of so much of their material that failed to sit well in the increasingly large arenas they are playing. Maybe Chris' lack of confidence was still evident. Whatever the reason, unlike their almost universally applauded recorded output, Coldplay's live shows have received some negative coverage such as this piece in *The Brain Farm* magazine: "To my ears, they still don't have enough tunes to cut it live... after a while the tunes did seem to blend into each other. 'Sparks' drags on and on, so does 'We Never Change'. A few others work, but it's all (too) relentlessly one-paced to make a real impact. At the moment, they're still finding their feet."

CHAPTER 14:

GOING ROUND THE BENDS

The Top Five placing of *A Rush...* in the *Billboard* charts was no doubt helped by the success of Radiohead's awkward recent album *Kid A* and their previous smash hit album, *OK Computer*. The Oxford-based band and Coldplay have often been cvompared to one another, and it is worth dwelling on the similarities a little further.

Like Coldplay, Thom Yorke's outfit also met at an educational establishment, albeit much earlier – Thom met guitarist Colin Greenwood at Secondary School aged only fourteen. The speed of the band's progress was much slower than Coldplay's too – it wasn't until five years later that the Radiohead line-up solidified and they played their first gig at the Jericho Tavern in their hometown. Whereas Coldplay "borrowed" their name, Radiohead started off with the rather amateur-sounding On A Friday, but thankfully changed this soon after, albeit taking the moniker from a strange reggae track on the Talking Heads' *True Stories* album. Instead of a friend managing them, their pal handed the tape to former musician Chris Hufford at a local studio who promptly took on the role of manager.

Like Coldplay, Radiohead signed to EMI after numerous gigs and much record label interest, although the latter signed their deal after only recording a demo, not with the benefit of a handful of independent releases as with Coldplay. Radiohead's March 1992 *Drill EP* charted at number 101, even lower than Coldplay's 'Brothers And Sisters', and likewise prompted the Oxford band to similarly look for new producers (their manager Hufford had produced the EP).

Unlike Coldplay, Radiohead's début album was completed in just three weeks. Unlike Coldplay, it did not reach number one nor did it turn the band into megastars almost overnight. However, like Coldplay, it did contain Radiohead's own 'Yellow'. The track was called 'Creep' but it failed to attract either the sales or critical acclaim of Coldplay's 'Yellow'. Instead the 6,000 UK sales of the single (getting it to number 78 rather than number five for the latter) and modest reviews suggested Radiohead would only ever be moderate achievers. However, like 'Yellow', the single became a huge radio smash in the US and this turned everything around for Radiohead. And like 'Yellow', 'Creep' brought such unexpected pressure on Radiohead that for a while there was a very real chance that the band would never make it intact to the second album.

It was just as well they did, because unlike Coldplay, Radiohead's début album *Pablo Honey* was simply not strong enough to make turn them into one of the world's biggest bands. The protracted tour that the success of 'Creep' forced the band to undertake left them, like Chris Martin, bereft of time and inspiration for new material. When the second album sessions started, morale was pitifully low and there was genuine concern for the band's survival. After some aborted sessions, the band toured down under before returning, energised to complete the album in two weeks.

> "Thom Yorke ignored me at a hotel in Los Angeles. I was secretly a bit gutted. I always look at it like we're in a big musical high school and Radiohead is in the year above us"

While Coldplay were allowed no time to grow up in public, being thrust into such an intense spotlight with their very first album, Radiohead waited until their sophomore effort to make that break. The record was called *The Bends* and for Radiohead it changed *everything*.

Instead of being seen as a whimsical, sometimes odd pop/rock band, *The Bends* revealed the far deeper and more complex songwriting genius that was at work within Radiohead. It particularly showcased Thom Yorke and enigmatic guitarist Johnny Greenwood's talents. Although an album behind Coldplay, Radiohead were now seen as very genuine contenders in the world of rock and like the former were quickly filling larger venues across the world.

Unlike Coldplay, it wasn't until a later single from the album, 'Street Spirit (Fade Out)', that the public really caught on to the band. While Coldplay have enjoyed profile almost from their very first major release, Radiohead were finally reaping the rewards of years and years of hard work.

The musical comparison with Coldplay really comes to the fore with this understated and quite beautiful second Radiohead album. However, their third album, the epochal *OK Computer*- now a regularly highly placed on any 'Best Album Ever' list - sees Radiohead begin to mark out their territory as one of the world's most experimental and unique bands. While songs such as 'Clocks' and 'Politik' do remind the listener of much of this third Radiohead album, particularly the crashing climaxes and crescendos of noise, there are far more reference points to *A Rush...* than just these two Radiohead albums.

Also, Coldplay have yet to make a habit of writing songs that last eight minutes or longer. Coldplay also had the pressure of a deadline for their second album while Radiohead were told to hand in the third album only when they were

RADIOHEAD

ready. On a more superficial note, Chris even wears an elastic bandage on his wrist when playing the guitar, because of repetitive strain pains, but obviously this leads to inevitable comparisons with the contraption worn by Johnny Greenwood.

Radiohead have enjoyed similar critical acclaim to Coldplay, sharing numerous awards including a Grammy for 'Best Alternative Album'. Much of their attention focuses on singer/writer Thom Yorke, who is a shy, elusive and peculiarly brilliant frontman. Coldplay's Jon Buckland is admired by many for his individuality and idiosyncratic experimentalism – likewise Radiohead guitarist Johnny Greenwood.

Both bands regularly express their disdain at press intrusion and acknowledge the absurdity of their job and position. Both band's videos are also acclaimed – the similarities between the impact of the promo clips for 'The Scientist' and 'No Surprises' has already been discussed. Both bands also support various charities such as Amnesty International and numerous children's charities.

Like Coldplay, Radiohead fiercely control every aspect of their career. They design the artwork themselves although it has to be said it is far more obscure and at times pretentious than the sleeves for *Parachutes* and *A Rush...*

Like Coldplay, Radiohead have enjoyed success in America, to date far more than Chris Martin's outfit. *OK Computer* was a number one album in America and the band already play stadiums over there, a benchmark Coldplay have yet to reach.

Nonetheless, it would be fascinating to see if Coldplay follow Radiohead's footsteps and veer off into the deeply peculiar vein of avante-garde music that saw them produce the uncommercial but critically acclaimed albums *Kid A* (another US number one and another Grammy winner) and *Amnesiac*. Certainly there are signs from Coldplay's second album that the band is not happy to deliver simple three-minute ballads ad infinitum. Yet it is Radiohead's instinct to hurtle into such unorthodox waters that has opened up the vacuum for a new melancholy guitar band that Coldplay are perfectly suited to fill. Whether they can evolve like Radiohead, to become the historically important rock band that they have, remains to be seen.

One final point about all this musical semantics. To be fair, bands so often moan about comparisons being made and, worse still, come out with phrases such as "our music isn't really like anyone else's" or "don't pigeon-hole us", but they misinterpret the intentions of the magazines who do this. After all, these magazine writers are bombarded with hundreds of new bands each year and have to describe and translate to their readers what each one sounds like. Without referring to other bands, this would be virtually impossible.

The problem is exacerbated by the fact that bands become overly precious about it all. Coldplay are probably wise to try to avoid this pigeon-hole – as mentioned it can sometimes prove suffocating - but ultimately they will be judged by their own musical output and if that is not good enough, then no amount of positive comparisons with any band will save them.

As a final note on the subject, when Chris eventually came across Radiohead's frontman, the occasion was a huge disappointment, as he told *Entertainment Weekly*: "Thom Yorke ignored me at a hotel in Los Angeles. I was secretly a bit gutted. I'm sure he recognized me. I always look at it like we're in a big musical high school and Radiohead is in the year above us and they still haven't come and sat with us at lunch."

CHRIS WITH MO MOWLAM

CHAPTER 15:

SNEAKING IN THROUGH THE (SLIDING) DOORS

Coldplay's success has inevitably brought about a relentless media interest in their private lives, particularly that of Chris Martin. Of specific fascination is Chris' relationship with winsome Hollywood actress Gwyneth Paltrow. Famed for the tearful Oscar acceptance speech, Gwyneth has inadvertently introduced the new Millennial term of "doing a Gwyneth" into the lexicon. New York-raised Paltrow is five years Chris' senior, close friends with Madonna and the McCartney daughters and mixes in the very highest echelons of the Hollywood A-list jet-set. So how did this bizarre coupling come about?

Gwyneth was first spotted at US Coldplay shows in early 2001, but it seems it wasn't until the show at New York's Bowery Ballroom in autumn 2002 that they actually met on more personal terms. Since then it was suggested that Gwyneth had been to every Coldplay gig including both the Brits and Grammys.

At first, Chris laughed off suggestions of an affair. He said that if he stood next to comedian Les Dennis, the paparazzi would be interested only in photos of the latter. He pointed out that he was also supposed to be dating Natalie Imbruglia. "It's really mad, fame. Should I sue them? I was really pissed off with them because it's not true. The only person I've ever been pictured embracing in public was Mo Mowlam and I'm fine with that." Another rumoured relationship with the quirky Nelly Furtado was apparently over as soon as it had (allegedly) started. Again this was strenuously denied.

Previously Chris' relationships had been very low profile, even soliciting the man himself to admit he was "a loser in all things romantic", with some of the less than sensitive tabloids pointing out this "self-confessed nerd" had only lost his virginity aged 22 (he had mentioned this to a journalist, regretted it immediately and asked for it not to be printed). This admission in the music press was a small slip-up but it was magnified a thousandfold when *The Sun* splashed the story across its 'showbiz' pages the following week.

GWYNETH PALTROW

Gwyneth, of course, was no stranger to the world of tabloid journalism. Only recently she had bemoaned the intrusions of the paparazzi rifling through her garbage, claiming paper shredders had been invented "for girls like me". She had also ironically just declared that British men never asked her out. Although she later seemed to retract this statement, claiming she had been misquoted, it made it seem all the more peculiar that she was now purported to be dating Chris Martin, a quiet, shy Englishman. Naturally, she wouldn't commit, saying, "I don't read any newspaper that has any gossip in it. I read *The Financial Times*. I don't really know what (the tabloids) think and what they say."

Nonetheless, the next thing Coldplay fans saw were pictures of Chris running from a car, hunched under in increasingly larger woolly hats, into Gwyneth's London home. Tabloid bibles such as *Heat* tagged onto the latest celebrity couple like a magnet. With Posh and Becks keeping a low profile after the horrific kidnap threats against Victoria Beckham and their children, plus Justin Timberlake and Britney Spears having split, not everyone wanted to read about Michael Douglas and Catherine Zeta-Jones suing *OK!* for £1 million. Ever hungry, the spotlight scanned elsewhere in celebrity land and, alighting on Gwyneth's beauty and Chris' current acclaim, elevated the pair to the level where a trip to the supermarket becomes front-page news. It seemed that at first even Chris couldn't help notice the apparent incongruity of the match: "She's a big Hollywood star and I'm just the bloke from Coldplay."

But this was hardly a real life *Notting Hill*. The extent of Coldplay' critical adulation had extended into the realm of celebrity applause too, not least with the band's ever-growing guest list of superstars. Chris was also beginning a wining streak of 'World's Sexiest Man' awards. So this was not exactly a beauty and the beast, no Monroe and Miller. There were other reasons to suggest the relationship was entirely plausible too. Both were known for their clean-living and both had enjoyed somewhat privileged upbringings. Also, Gwyneth made no secret of the fact she found much of her celebrity life nauseating.

Gwyneth was still reeling from the loss of her father from throat cancer in 2001 and it seemed that this new relationship had really taken her by welcome surprise. By October 2002, the veil of secrecy seemed to have slipped away. At Coldplay's second Wembley Arena show in that month, midway through their encore, Chris dedicated 'In My Place' to Gwyneth. He didn't say he was her boyfriend, and he also dedicated several songs to his mother who was in the crowd, but this was nonetheless a recognition that a relationship of sorts existed. This was fuelled when Gwyneth was also spotted at the Dublin show of this same set of dates.

By the start of November 2002, UK tabloids had squeezed even more out of him. He admitted to having been on dates with Gwyneth but denied that they were yet an item. In a eulogy that must have had Alan McGee steaming at the ears, he said to *The Sun*, "I'm proud to be with someone who's very nice and very beautiful but she's not my girlfriend at the moment. I feel out of my depth with all this. I met her for the first time at our gig at Wembley two weeks ago. It's early days. I got her number, rang her and asked if she wanted to meet.

We went out at the weekend and we seem to get on… I don't know when we're going out again. I feel uncomfortable talking about her. We're just becoming friends."

By now the rumour mill was in full operation. Gwyneth was reported to be so smitten with Chris that she flew her mother, Blythe Danner, to a party at Sting and wife Trudie Styler's house just to meet her new beau. *Heat* magazine even went as far as to get bookies odds of 2-1 on the Paltrow/Martin pairing as "favourite celebrity couple to get married this year". Others made comparisons to Madonna and Guy Ritchie, a similar duo of public-school educated Brit and high profile US star.

Despite having been dating only four months, the pair spent Christmas and New Year's Eve together at the Martin family home in Devon, a splendid nineteenth century manor house. In a scene straight out of pretty much any Hugh Grant film, Chris was even seen buying Ms Paltrow a pint at his local pub, The Royal Oak in Nadderwater ('Good Food, Fine Ales'). Not exactly The Ivy, but Gwyneth seemed not to care. Nor did she mind going to see Chris' eleven-year-old sister in panto.

> "I definitely don't feel ready to have (kids) right now. I love not working. I love sleeping late and just, you know, doing yoga and hanging out. It's just great."

Switching continents, the pair flew to Los Angeles for the New Year with Gwyneth's mother, albeit after checking in separately to avoid prying eyes. Despite such subterfuge, Chris' guitar case was clearly spotted on Gwyneth's luggage trolley so the cover-up was rather unconvincing.

Then of course, according to the press, who seemed unduly pleased, it was all over. Six months after the news had started to break of a relationship, the February 2003 tabloids announced Gwyneth had ended the affair. Reports suggested that her previously troubled love life had left her determined not to be dumped and have her heart broken again – having seen former boyfriends Ben Affleck and Brad Pitt both end their relationship first. Unnamed "friends" said she had "toughened up" and that she only ever saw Chris as "an in-between' lover". Other anonymous sources suggested that Chris was "happy being single before he met Gwyneth, but she really has cast a spell on him and he seems ready to settle down."

Chris kept a dignified silence during much of this but did offer a few snippets of altogether confusing thoughts. At the *NME* Awards ceremony he told the press pack that "I am dating Julia Roberts" while another reporter who asked him about Paltrow was informed, "I don't know the girl, I've never even met her."

No one seemed quite certain if the affair was indeed over for a while but then magazines started running features again, such as 'Sizzling Snoggin' Snaps'. Gwyneth was said to have moved into Chris' north London flat; Chris was seen affectionately hugging her on set of her new movie, *Ted And Sylvia*; they spent the entire Valentine weekend together and, again only rumour, they were said to be attending the Oscars together. In the event, they didn't but only because the Oscar ceremony was deliberately subdued in light of the war with Iraq. For once the newspapers had something really important to splash on their front pages.

Notably, the juggernaut of Coldplay's success that followed the release of *A Rush Of Blood To The Head* was by now so weighty that reporters were asking Gwyneth is *she* felt insecure in the relationship, bearing in mind Chris's new found status as one of showbiz's premier men. By contrast, she remained very cagey about Chris when pressed about children and the future: "I definitely don't feel ready to have (kids) right now. I love not working. I love sleeping late and just, you know, doing yoga and hanging out. It's just great."

On or off, engaged or not, the ultra-high profile of the Chris/Gwyneth relationship is final proof, if it was needed, of Coldplay's ascent – or perhaps descent - into celebrity hell. Perhaps only Chris was the man the paparazzi wanted to photograph – the other three band members private lives have remained exactly that (the most revealing fact was that Jon was at one point close to an American lady he had met while the band were appearing on *Saturday Night Live*) – but nonetheless, the band were now faced at every gig and appearance with flash bulbs and press scrums. After taking such a mauling from Alan McGee and clearly struggling to come to terms with his new found place in the spotlight only a couple of years earlier, it remains to be seen if a more media-savvy Chris will be able to handle this even greater pressure with more aplomb and ease. Let's hope so, because by Will's own admission, without Chris in a positive frame of mind, there is no Coldplay.

CHAPTER 16:

WHEN WILL
WE BE KINGS?

While the UK tabloids had obsessed about Chris and Gwyneth's closeness, the band were busy reinforcing their US profile. The dates in support of *A Rush...* certainly had their fair share of surprises. In September, 2002, determined to avoid a repeat of the earlier cancelled US gigs, the band were faced with yet another disaster after a freak wind storm blew the roof off a venue in Atlanta. Chris and Jon promptly set up in the venue's car park and played a surprise and avidly received mini-set to a delighted crowd. Ash, who was supporting Coldplay on these dates, also played an indoor replacement gig that night by way of further compensation. For their tracks 'Kung Fu' and 'Shining Light', Chris joined them on vocals.

In February, 2003, Coldplay announced that their next US gig would be the 20,000-seat Madison Square Garden, final confirmation that they were a serious player on the American music scene. This commercial success in the USA was complemented by the news that *A Rush...* had been nominated for two Grammys, namely 'Best Alternative Music Album' and 'Best Rock Performance By Duo or Group With Vocals' for the single 'In My Place'. Having flown by Concorde the night after the Brits to the ceremony, the 'Best Alternative Music Album' Grammy triumphantly went to Coldplay. On the night they performed live alongside other acts including Bruce Springsteen and Nelly (whose 'Hot In Herre' (sic) they had covered once in New York). America, it seemed, was theirs for the taking.

The UK, of course, had already fallen. They played 'Clocks' on stage and dominated the February 2003 Brit Awards, most notably with 'Best Band' and 'Best Album' gongs, but the highlight of the night came when the camera panned over to where they were sitting to capture their reactions on hearing of yet another win, only to inexplicably find Chris on the stairway, posterior in the air and legs akimbo. He was on particularly good form and it seemed as though Coldplay and their enigmatic frontman had finally come to terms with what they represented and what that entailed.

The campaign continued in January 2003 with a raft of yet more North American dates, 33 in total, which was extended well into March due to ticket demand. They then returned to Europe for eleven more shows, before flying to the UK for some arena dates in mid-April, at the Manchester Evening News Arena and the cavernous Earls Court in London. These three shows – their biggest indoor shows ever in the UK, will be preceded by their smallest, when they play a live session in front of just thirty people for BBC Radio 1's *Mark and Lard Show*. Then it was back out to America for yet more shows. The year of massive gigs – final confirmation if any was needed that Coldplay were now a stadium band – continued with news that they were to headline V2003 alongside Red Hot Chilli Peppers. By March, 2003, they had already sold 4.5 million copies of *A Rush…*, a quite remarkable achievement. It was only a matter of time before these sales figures surged past those for *Parachutes*.

> "I'm still getting used to seeing pictures of myself and hearing my voice on the radio, it's a strange thing to get used to. I am a pretty shy guy and I prefer to be anonymous. I love music but I never wanted to be a rock star" CHRIS

There were even a few signs of new material, suggesting that this time around Chris was not finding writing as difficult as he had between the first and second albums. On the same day that 'The Scientist' entered the singles charts, Coldplay performed at The Royal Albert Hall in aid of the Teenage Cancer Trust, where two new songs were aired, namely 'Gravity' and a very rocky number called 'Marianne'.

Although the two had previously appeared to get on, at this show Oasis' Liam Gallagher took a direct swipe at both Chris and Gwyneth after the band made it known they were intensely anti-war. After both singers appeared at a series of concerts in aid of children with cancer at the Royal Albert Hall in Kensington, Liam took exception to what he felt was Chris using the event as a platform: "When Coldplay did this gig they banged on about the war, that's wrong. Chris Martin shouldn't be using this cause to bang on about his own views on the war.

If him and his gawky bird want to go banging on about the war they can do it at their own gigs. That lot are just a bunch of knobhead students – Chris Martin looks like a geography teacher. What's all that with writing messages about Free Trade on his hand? If he wants to write things down I'll give him a pen and a pad of paper. Bunch of students. These gigs are about kids who have got cancer, they've got to fight a war every day of their lives. That's what we're all here doing this for." Despite this, many people in the crowd stood and applauded Chris when he encouraged them to "sing against the war."

What the future holds for Coldplay is anyone's guess. They were rumoured to be starring in Ash's supposed horror feature film, *Slashed*, along with other tour mates of the Irish band such as Moby, The Hives, The Vines, Dave Grohl and Neil Hannon. Might Chris end up as an actor alongside his Oscar-winning girlfriend? It seems unlikely.

A solo career for Chris would certainly be the focus of much attention, but whether he would follow in the muted steps of The Verve's Richard Ashcroft or seize the opportunity and become even bigger than Coldplay remains to be seen. If he goes solo at all, of course, of which there has never been any suggestion of such from the band.

Chris, however, was starting to look around at different musical experiences than just Coldplay. He had found time to record a duet with a favourite of his, Canadian singer songwriter Ron Sexsmith. Their version of the country ballad

'Gold In Them Hills' was captured on tape at London's Electric Earth East Studios in mid-2002, and penned in to appear as a bonus track on Sexmith's fifth album *Cobblestone Runway*. Hardly the beginnings of a solo career, however.

Guy had already revealed plans to work with US rockers At The Drive-In on a country-influenced record in El Paso, more specifically with Drive-In guitarist Jim, under the name London Country Rebels. "It's funny," said Guy, 'but we both hate people who think we shouldn't like other kinds of music than the stuff we play. They're in it for the music and have so many things going on musically, and so do we." Having met that band while in Australia for The Big Day Out festival, it was a clear sign that individual members were already looking to broaden their musical horizons.

It seems highly unlikely that any of the other members might pursue a solo career, having made such a point of enjoying their closely protected private lives and relative privacy, as Will pointed out: "I don't feel famous at all. I like the way the name of the band is becoming more known, but I can put my hat on after a gig and slip into anonymity."

Will remains extremely optimistic about the future, as he mused in *The Observer*: "We all found that first year in Coldplay, with all the success and acclaim and criticism, bewildering. We didn't lose it, but we lost our bearings, probably Chris most of all. Now we've got a handle on it and we're confident about who we are. We all feel very excited about what we can do. There are limitless possibilities."

At the moment there appears to be no sign of Chris losing touch with reality, much to his credit. At a midnight record store opening in November 2002 to buy signed copies of David Gray's new album, the appropriately named *New Day At Midnight*, Chris turned up at the last minute and asked to buy five copies. When staff recognised him, they offered him free copies but he insisted on paying. When they refused his money, he gave them the equivalent amount of cash to go and buy some drinks for themselves instead.

Now that he appears acclimatised to his newly found rock star status (he now even enjoys giving autographs), there is every chance that Chris Martin and Coldplay's success will explode even further. The two are obviously inextricably linked and always will be. Inevitably, despite or rather because of the fanfare surrounding *A Rush...*

Chris is already making mental lists of concerns, as he told *X Ray* magazine: "We always worry about something, so we're worried about a backlash, or the next record, all that sort of stuff."

Critics can be quick to denigrate rock stars for finding their fame a strange bedfellow but if you consider that in the spring of 1999, Chris Martin was an aspiring musician without a major record deal and about to take his final degree exams. Within three years, he had sold millions of albums and was dating a woman who earned millions of dollars for every film she appeared in. Obviously the money, cars, acclaim, adulation and success temper his insecurities, but it is surely not as simple as one thinks. Kind of like the old bar room boast of "I'd get in a ring with Mike Tyson for $10 million". Question is, would you ever get out again?

Chris makes no secret of the fact he thinks he has "the greatest job in the world." He has said that a different twist of fate might have seen him playing "Elton John covers in Marriot Hotels up and down the country: 'Enjoy the buffet, this is 'Rocket Man.'"

With critical acclaim and commercial success already accomplished so early in the band's career, the problem for Chris Martin is surely going to be his relentless need to equal the greats, his desire to be on level terms – by his own admission – with legends such as McCartney. With such lofty ambitions, there is a distinct possibility that he might never be sated. Coldplay are rock royalty already, of that there is no doubt. But might Chris well be sitting on the throne already and not even realise?

DISCOGRAPHY

Coldplay have released numerous vinyl, CD and DVD formats
in various permutations of their singles throughout the globe.
This discography covers the releases in the UK with key alterations
to this schedule being covered in the main text.

ALBUMS

PARACHUTES

Don't Panic
Shiver
Spies
Sparks
Yellow
Trouble
Parachutes
High Speed
We Never Change
Everything's Not Lost

July 2000

A RUSH OF BLOOD TO THE HEAD

Politik
In My Place
God Put A Smile Upon Your Face
The Scientist
Clocks
Daylight
Green Eyes
Warning Sign
A Whisper
A Rush Of Blood To The Head
Amsterdam

August 2002

SINGLES

THE SAFETY EP
Bigger
Stronger
No More Keeping My Feet
  On The Ground
Such A Rush

1997, 500 copies only

BROTHERS AND SISTERS
Easy To Please
Only Superstition

May 1998, 2500 copies only

THE BLUE ROOM EP
Bigger
Stronger
Don't Panic
See You Soon
High Speed
Such A Rush

April 1999, 5000 copies only

SHIVER
For You
Careful Where You Stand

October 1999

YELLOW
Help Is Round The Corner
No More Keeping My Feet
  On The Ground

March 2000

TROUBLE
Brothers And Sisters
Shiver (acoustic version)

October 2000

IN MY PLACE
One I Love
I Bloom Blaum

August 2002

THE SCIENTIST
1.36
I Ran Away

November 2002

CLOCKS
Crests of Waves
Animals

March 2003